# Time and Time Again

-

# exploring past lives

by
Kayla Mackenzie-Kopp

Kororā Press, Waiheke Island

# Time and Time Again - exploring past lives

by Kayla Mackenzie-Kopp

Copyright 2015 Kayla Mackenzie-Kopp
All rights reserved. No part of this publication may be reproduced in any form or by any means without prior permission from the publisher.

Kororā Press
43 Kororā Rd, Oneroa, Waiheke Island 1081
New Zealand

www.kororapress.net

kororapress@gmail.com

e-book ISBN 978-0-473-33820-6

print ISBN 978-0-473-33819-0

Cover design by wwwdigitaldonna.com

All experiences recounted here can be vouched for, but names of some individuals have been changed to maintain their privacy.

*Thou hast made me endless, such is thy pleasure. This frail vessel thou emptiest again and again, and fillest it ever with fresh life.*
*This little flute of a reed thou hast carried over hills and dales, and hast breathed through it melodies eternally new.*
*At the immortal touch of thy hands my little heart loses its limits in joy and gives birth to utterance ineffable. Thy infinite gifts come to me only on these very small hands of mine. Ages pass, and still thou pourest, and still there is room to fill.*

**Rabindranath Tagore**

# Table of Contents

PREFACE........................................................................1

INTRODUCTION..........................................................3

CHAPTER 1 Childhood, Healing and Humility.........12

CHAPTER 2 Scars of Persecution..............................26

CHAPTER 3 Inner and Outer Space...........................35

CHAPTER 4 First Contact with Earth........................44

CHAPTER 5 Relationships and Jealousy...................56

CHAPTER 6 The Gift of Unconditional Love...........65

CHAPTER 7 Knowing the Mind, Knowing the Body 75

CHAPTER 8 Flying Neolithic Style............................85

CHAPTER 9 Scholarship versus Experience.............91

CHAPTER 10 Light and Darkness..............................96

CHAPTER 11 Leadership and Responsibility..........103

CHAPTER 12 Regression Transcript........................111

CHAPTER 13 Regression Technique.......................126

CHAPTER 14 Concluding Thoughts........................137

Books You May Find Helpful....................................140

About the Author.........................................................141

# PREFACE

The fact that we seldom have a conscious memory of our past lives doesn't mean they do not affect us now. What we are confronted with this time round is formed from the patterns created in the lives that preceded it. Knowing more about these patterns can add a wider perspective and understanding to our view of our current life. This was certainly the case for me. I find it hard to imagine how I would see my life without knowing the richness of other lives I have experienced.

It can be practically useful as well. In this context I think of my elder son in his teenage years. He was very good at all his classes except French. He failed every French exam, and seemed physically incapable of directing his attention to that subject - very strange for an otherwise highly intelligent and capable scholar.

In our despair about it I suggested doing a past life regression to the life which held the origin of his block about French. The story which came up in deep relaxation was of an American during World War II who was in France to liaise with the French resistance. Some network breakdown prevented him from contacting the French group who were expecting him, and he was caught by others. As he couldn't speak French, they thought he was German, and tortured him to death. He took on the belief that French was mortally dangerous. Towards the end of the session with me, my son was able to let go of that belief.

He passed every French exam after that.

I felt hesitant about publishing this book, which contains many private details from my life. However I've been persuaded to make it public, as it may be of value to others.

May the ideas in this book help you understand some of the challenges in your life, as they have helped me and people I have accompanied on these timeless journeys. May the book enrich your life in whatever way is right for you.

# INTRODUCTION

## Why Bother about Past Lives?

Let me tell you about a tool I use which has helped me to make more sense of my life. Perhaps it could make your life simpler, freer and more meaningful too.

The tool I am offering is my experience in working with past lives. You can choose to chip away at some of the problem areas in your own life with it, or discard it and reach for some other tool. Whatever you decide, I hope you enjoy this excursion into the mysterious territory of past lives.

This book does not attempt to prove the authenticity of past lives. So much research has been done already in this field that I will simply assume, since you are reading these words, that you are open to the idea of reincarnation, if not convinced of it.

Interestingly enough, you don't even have to believe in past lives to benefit from doing reincarnation therapy. If you like, you can see past life work as a very fast way of discovering in symbolic form our subconscious patterns. You can, if you wish, look at the material that surfaces as being similar to the impressions that our subconscious mind gives us during dreams.

For many of us, however, the impressions have a vividness and sense of truth to them which convince us that we are actually reviewing past lives. There is an authenticity and a depth of insight which cannot be denied. And many of the past life memories collected worldwide have been verified by later research.

If you have never thought much about the possibility of having past lives, however, you may well be asking yourself what the point is in bothering about them. Haven't we got enough to do trying to deal with the life we're living? That's just it. Looking at past lives can often help us deal with our current life more easily. Why else would we look at them?

It would also seem that as we progress on our path through this life, as we become more aware of ourselves as spirit living in matter, the realization that we have lived before and will live again becomes more and more obvious. Choosing consciously to look at past lives can be a fast and effective way towards becoming freer and more whole now.

It can help us understand and let go of some of our destructive behavioural patterns, our horizons can become much wider, and we can appreciate life without being quite so obsessed with the story we are living out at the moment. Past life work is a useful tool - if it feels

# INTRODUCTION

appropriate to you to use it, that option is open to you. It can enrich and liberate your life greatly.

Most of the people who come to me with the wish to investigate their earlier existences are motivated by an issue in their current life which they cannot explain by looking at their everyday experiences. This issue may be a physical one such as lameness or chronic ill health, a psychological one such as their fear of speaking in public or their inability to make decisions, or an interpersonal one, for example, their conflict with a partner or parent. Doing a regression may be a powerful way of releasing the blockages which are hindering a harmonious life, especially if other methods have brought little relief.

Gaining awareness of past lives seems to be a natural by-product of spiritual development. Gautama Buddha, for example, is said to have witnessed all his past lives again as he entered into enlightenment. It could be that probing our more ancient past, if the urge is there, speeds up our "progress". By "progress" I mean our ability to lose our attachment to our current ego and personality, and to find instead, with a deep compassion, an awareness of the oneness of all life.

On the way to this all-encompassing awareness, past-life work can help with the simplifying of the individual and the dissolving of unhelpful programming. If people vividly re-experience that they have been man and woman, perpetrator and victim, ruler and ruled, black and white, saint and sinner, then they can stop pointing their finger at others, and clear up their own lives instead. If, at some time or other, we have lived in most of the cultures on earth, what is the point of being aggressively patriotic about the country we are living in this time round? If we have adhered to most of the major religious traditions at some time or other, why not accept that all paths lead us back to the divine? As we work on ourselves through investigating past lives and letting go of the drama in their stories, true compassion can begin to grow.

It seems probable that if more people on earth realized that the drama they are currently living is their own production, they would stop complaining and judging, and start loving, accepting, forgiving and clearing up. They would also realise that creating new karmic entanglements is foolish. Were we really to accept this realization, most sources of conflict on earth could disappear. It seems almost too simple to be true.

It is helpful to think of the patterns of our emotional reactions as if they are software which has been installed in the "computer" of our brains and the cells of our bodies during emotionally charged moments in this or other lives. We react according to the software that has been installed; we feel according to the emotional programming which has been imprinted in our minds and in our cells. This imprinting is the stuff through which karma (cause and effect) is played out – until we learn to release the karma.

## INTRODUCTION

Working with past lives can be an effective way to gain insight into how the laws of karma work. And having understood more about that, and released some of the programming we have believed in for centuries, we can come to the point when we can let go of the necessity of karma. This requires, of course, understanding on a deep level; simple acknowledgement of an extended horizon as a mental exercise does not bring about this shift in consciousness. We are, however, infinitely more than our personal identity in this life. Bringing that awareness into everyday life can bring us nearer to oneness with all that is.

Just as we can work on neutralizing some of the childhood programming that is so effectively, and often so destructively, running our lives now, we can also work on even older programming - for example, that which is the source of the childhood experiences.

Each time we incarnate, our cells encode the experiences we have had at other times. The more emotionally charged the past events, the more indelible the imprint, even though the conscious memory of the events is seldom present. Many of these cellular memories may serve us in our development. Others may hold us back from manifesting our true potential now. Using past life regressions, we have the possibility of looking at old traumas and seeing what we may have been trying to learn as we chose to experience that way. We can let go of the held-over emotional shock which has been binding us to a prescribed form of reaction that no longer serves us. Similarly, we can consciously call up past experiences which may enrich our lives now.

I am talking about "past" lives even though I am aware that time is an illusion. However in the world of matter in which we appear to live, time is a component we consider valid. That is the way we experience life here on earth at present. So I will talk about "past lives" as if they existed chronologically.

If you would like a scientific explanation of how energy is passed on from life to life, read Dr Bruce Lipton's book *The Biology of Belief* (it's in the book list at the end of this book).

Nowadays, there is a huge amount of research available to the student of reincarnation, which verifies the "stories" or "memories" of past lives. In the practical reincarnation work that I have done, however, I have never made an effort to verify the facts of any of the regressions. I have been simply looking for emotional and spiritual insight for myself or for the hundreds of others I have worked with. The regressions have been primarily a therapeutic tool. I realize that in a majority of these cases there is no "proof" that what I or another person is experiencing as a past life is anything more than a figment of the imagination, a product of the subconscious mind, comparable to a dream. But why, we can ask ourselves, do we have this particular dream rather than some other one?

# INTRODUCTION

There is also the possibility that we are somehow tuning in to collective memories of mankind – and surely clearing the emotional charge from that would also be a service for all.

Although neither I nor any of my clients have ever seen ourselves as well-known historical characters (with one exception, which I have not included here) it's common enough to hear stories about people who consider themselves to be incarnations of some famous person, such as Jesus of Nazareth or Cleopatra. We could say that the person making such claims is simply deluded. However maybe there is another explanation. It could be that such beings had a particularly strong energy field, some aspect of which resonates with a part of the personality of the person who claims they are their next incarnation. Although it seems obvious to others that they do not carry the presence of that famous person, their ego clings to the associated glamour.

Although I have never made any attempt to prove the historical correctness of regressions I have done, I have often been impressed that something I have reported on during a regression to some ancient culture can be verified when I later read information about that culture. I can also recognise landscapes which I have never visited before in this life.

When investigating my own past lives and when working as a reincarnation therapist with others, I generally use the method taught to me by my friend and teacher, Rhea Powers.

In the eighties, I participated in Europe in the "Lightwork" training courses, which were run by Rhea and her then husband, Gawain Bantle. The "Lightwork" courses covered several years of intense spiritual training. One of the components of the courses was past life work. After completing the training courses, I began working as a therapist in this field, and have since trained other therapists to work this way, as well as accompanying Rhea as a translator and assistant in a number of courses. Naturally my own experience and growth has added my own "flavour" to Rhea`s foundation.

In Chapter 13 I give a brief outline of the method I use when accompanying someone in a regression. I do this from a therapist's perspective although most of the collection of "lives" that forms the rest of this book are from my own experience. The simple reason for this was that I had no detailed records of most of my client's past life journeys. I just made a few notes at the end of the session with them, which was enough of a reminder at the time. If you are not interested in the method, ignore Chapter 13.

It is necessary for your understanding of what follows, however, for you to know now that after someone goes through the life they have regressed to, and then briefly experiences their death in it, they expand into the light

## INTRODUCTION

and become one with their Higher Self or soul. It is here that healing takes place and the person finally comes to understand what that life was really about. Merely looking at the past life does not heal the soul, but the higher perspective can. In the "concluding comments" of each chapter, I often mention the insights found at this higher level, along with the practical influence the regression had in my life.

I wish you joyful insight.

## CHAPTER 1

## Childhood, Healing and Humility

As far back as I can remember, I have been drawn to the world of the spirit. That is probably why I became a reincarnation therapist. Perhaps that awareness of other dimensions came about because I died immediately after my birth, and was resuscitated.

According to my mother, I was then hung upside down from the ceiling for three days to drain the water out of my lungs, while she battled for her life on the intensive ward. I can remember going into a sort of limbo of empty blackness in those days, purposely not being present anywhere. I can also remember an angel saying to me at the moment of that brief death, "You must go back to your body. You chose this life. But we will give you all the flowers of the earth as comfort." It smiled at me with measureless tenderness, and then I can remember the sweetness and warmth of breast milk.

My parents were theosophists, so from childhood on my sisters and I were taken rather unwillingly to

## Childhood, Healing and Humility

theosophical lectures on comparative religion, philosophy and science. I didn't like most of the talks, but having a warm drink of Milo and some biscuits when we got home made up for them. Most of the talks I found rather boring because the style of speech of many of the lecturers made them seem like dry, dusty books on legs. Having to listen to them did mean, however, that I was conversant from an early age with the logic behind the theory of reincarnation, and it seemed the only sensible explanation to me for the differences in the circumstances which people were born into and the "unfair" distribution of talents they had brought with them.

Harry Banks, the clairvoyant Liberal Catholic bishop, was someone who furthered my impulse towards spiritual things. He was a theosophist too, and during my childhood he came to stay with us from time to time. He was very small, not much bigger than a child himself, with very pink skin and a frill of silky white hair around the edges of his head. We used to sit on his knee, and he'd tell us stories about fairies. He brought us little wooden elephants from India. I told him that I'd seen someone on a cloud who looked like Jesus with a purple cloak. He said I was lucky, and we would see if it happened again, but it didn't.

We became part of Bishop Banks' "Golden Chain" group, which had a prayer beginning "I am a link in the golden chain of love which stretches round the world, and I shall keep my link bright and strong… So I shall try to think pure and beautiful thoughts, to speak pure and beautiful words and to do pure and beautiful actions." I can't remember how it went on after that.

My parents didn't talk about the Bible at all, but they did send us to Sunday School at a nearby church, and they gave me a Bible. At the front of my Bible was a picture of Jesus knocking at a door. I think it was entitled "Is anyone within?" and someone told me Jesus was knocking at our hearts to see if we'd hear Him. I was fascinated by the picture and wondered if I'd notice if He knocked at my heart, and what would happen if I didn't hear Him. I lay in bed at night entertaining myself by making my hands take on a blessing gesture (two fingers up, two down, as in a Byzantine temple), and then making them look clawlike, like a devil's hand, which scared me, so I went back to the blessing hand.

In bed at a very young age I also used to hold my hand about six inches away from my head, keeping my eyes closed. Then I would pass my hand back and forth in front of my forehead. I always knew when my hand passed in front of my third eye (though I didn't know what to call it then), as the movement of my hand set off an energy corkscrew which spiralled its way into my forehead. I was intrigued by the sensation. I can also remember feeling that I was enormously large, and trying to squeeze myself into my body, which felt much too small. It was like trying to push a large piece of foam rubber into a matchbox. I knew very well that I was more than my body, but I never talked to anyone about these things.

When I was small there were three things I wanted to be "when I grew up". One was a mother (because I loved my mother), one was an animal doctor (an idea a lady on a train talked me out of by explaining that vets spent most of their time artificially inseminating cows), and one was a saint. I wasn't sure what a saint was. I just knew they were very holy and close to God, and helped people. I never told anyone about wanting to be a saint, but I secretly practised my "blessing gesture", and I thought how beautiful it must be to touch someone and heal them.

I could not bear the thought of suffering. When I was six it broke my heart when the neighbour's cat, which had apparently eaten rat poison, came to me desperately ill, and then died with its head on my lap, my tears wetting its fur. I felt devastatingly helpless, and could not understand why God had let the cat suffer and die.

Not being able to ask God, I asked my mother. She couldn't find a reason that made sense to me, but she loved me unconditionally in my crisis, which warmed my heart. She suggested I ask my father for his explanation, as he was more versed in spiritual matters. There was no way I was going to turn to him, however, as he seemed cold and strict to me, and I could not imagine opening my wounded heart to him. So I pondered such things deeply in myself. When I look back, it seems that a kind of solemnity lay about me.

I spent a rather lonely childhood in Waimate and Timaru, and then we moved to Samoa for four years, where my father was a teacher. Here too I was often alone, being the only palangi in my class. I spent a lot of time reading books up trees, and watching animals.

On our return to New Zealand we moved to Hamilton, where my sisters and I continued learning music, though it was only my younger sister, Annette, on her cello who showed great talent. I didn't enjoy having to practise my violin, but later, when I was studying in Auckland, I joined the Auckland Junior Symphony Orchestra and played chamber music with other students. By then I was glad my parents had kept me to it.

I studied for a B.A. at Auckland University, taking German as my foreign language. Little did I know that this language choice would eventually lead me to spend a large portion of my life in Germany. After completing my degree, I set off to visit Europe, and through a series of surprising coincidences, ended up being offered a job as a *Lektorin* (junior lecturer) at the English Department of Heidelberg University – I hadn't even applied for the job! I remained on the staff of Heidelberg University for the next thirty three years, married and raised three children.

## Childhood, Healing and Humility

It was the trauma of my divorce, when my sons were eight and four respectively, that set me firmly back on my spiritual path. My life seemed to be spiralling out of control and I agonised about the suffering the divorce was causing my beloved children. As I was the only member of my family in Europe at that time, I had no support from relatives. Being a solo mum I felt more alone than ever.

Many people take up their conscious spiritual journey in an attempt to heal themselves and make life more manageable, and so it was with me. For years I attended seminars in spiritual growth and studied healing modalities. My experiences in these fields were hugely important to me, and I began passing on what I had learned and experienced to others. Healing in its wider sense became part of my professional life.

While I was teaching English at Heidelberg University, I established a part time practice offering a spiritual approach to psychotherapy. Among other things, I started working with people on their past lives. I also did "clearings" of unwanted energies from clients' energy fields. The energies I helped remove were sometimes emotional imprints, and sometimes souls who had remained earth-bound after their death and had attached themselves to someone. I also began experimenting with the energies of the chakras and their affect on people's health.

# TIME AND TIME AGAIN

Although I was working in this way in the healing arena, I didn't feel fully confident, and worried that my work might not be effective enough. This motivated me to do this regression to the past life which held my closest connection to healing.

## *Past Life Experience*

*I enter the life as a twenty year old woman, living and learning in the large round temple of the Mother which adorns the hill behind the capital of Atlantis. The temple is constructed from blocks of stone and is several stories high, growing narrower towards the top, and roofed with a dome. It dominates the town from its place on the hill, and has wide curving steps leading up to the main entrance.*

*I have lived here for three years already and am being trained in the healing arts. I have waving, dark hair, and wear a simple, white toga-like garment.*

*Every neophyte has to work in her first year in the domestic department where she must toil very hard cleaning, scrubbing, preparing food, washing the garments of the sisters, and generally being like a slave to the more advanced students. I hate this heavy work. It seems as if I have the two-toned pattern of the temple's marble floors engraved in the cellular memory of my hands and knees from the endless hours I have spent scrubbing them.*

## Childhood, Healing and Humility

*In that first year we are only occasionally allowed to join in the rituals and ceremonies of the whole sisterhood. I see us standing on a plateau on the hillside at dawn, dressed for the ceremony in different colours according to the level we are at in our training, following the Mother with our voices as she invokes the presence of Oneness as a blessing for all. These rare chances to share in the spiritual work of the community are like glimpses of heaven for me – at last I feel as if I am doing what it is natural for me to do. However I hide my pride and do my menial work and at last the year is up, a new influx of trainees arrive, and I and most of my class are allowed to move up to the second floor.*

*Here we learn the use of plants for healing. We gain the freedom to spend wonderful days out in the hills collecting herbs. When we bring our harvest back we learn how to dry, heat and pulverize it making essences, oils, tinctures and ointments. We are allowed to be present when patients are being treated, and are occasionally sent out to bring medicine to people in the town.*

*Many of the tasks with the herbs must be done at special phases of the moon or times of day. Sunrise is particularly potent, and I get up eagerly to do my work. I am intrigued and fulfilled by it and strive almost fanatically to do it immaculately well. When we take part in the celebrations and meditations in adoration of the Mother, I feel bathed in a sweetness and light which intoxicates me with its beauty.*

*In the third year we move on to the use of crystals and sound and energized water. I have a keen awareness of the energies, and am proud of my ability to sense them and to apply them in the healing not only of people but also of places. This year we are occasionally taught by the incarnation of the Mother herself. She is an elderly woman with waving white hair and a face so beautiful that I cannot take my eyes off her. Her eyes have so much knowledge, love and humour in them that we all adore her, though she can be as clear and hard as a diamond if she feels anyone has not applied herself with sufficient dedication.*

*I am convinced that I am one of the best students in our year and feel sure I will be selected to go on to the next level of training. Not all who have completed the training so far are considered suitable to continue, and indeed many do not wish to take the initiation required for the next stage. It consists of proving with the mind that the body is not bound by the normal laws of the elements. We must, for example, enter a darkened locked room with our mind, as if our body were in it, and describe in detail objects in the room, moving some of them.*

*This next level deals with the focussing and application of thought power, and those who are successful in it are*

## Childhood, Healing and Humility

*given the sword of judgement over life and death. I burn with the desire to excel here too.*

*My humiliation and incomprehension are boundless and agonizing when I am not one of those chosen to continue to the next level. I try reasoning with my beloved tutor, pointing out that my ability is well above most of the others. She says no-one doubts this, but she remains firm, saying that I must repeat the year I have just done until I have learnt humility.*

*Humility, humility – I hate humility! I can see no way in which humility will be useful to me in the challenges of wrestling with my mind and the minds of others. Burning with righteous indignation, shame, and zealous curiosity, I decide that whenever I can, I will glide soundlessly up to the next floor when teaching is going on, keep out of sight, and gather as much information as possible.*

*The first few times that I try this, lurking with pounding heart, all senses tensed, behind a pillar in the shadows, it seems to work. I return strangely exhausted and go about my work with the crystals as if nothing had happened.*

*On the fourth occasion my heart freezes with horror.*

*Sensing a change in the energy I turn and find the incarnation of the Mother standing before me. I had not heard her approach. "We have observed you," she says calmly, and her eyes see through my every*

# TIME AND TIME AGAIN

*pretence. "You have knowingly disobeyed us. You will return to working as a novice on the lowest floor. You may, if your progress is satisfactory, make another attempt to work your way up year by year."*

*"No!" I scream. "No! I curse your injustice!" I turn and race from the temple. I am no longer a member of the sisterhood.*

*The years that follow I spend living out all I did not live in the temple. It's as if I want to trample on my holy aspiration so as not to feel the pain of my exclusion. I have gained many skills in the temple which enable me to manipulate the emotions and thoughts of others effortlessly. I use these skills mercilessly to become one of the wealthiest and most influential women in the city. I play off my lovers against each other. My partners are powerful men, and I make use of their power to my own ends. I have a son, but even he disappoints me, having little of my fire and talent. I leave him mainly to my servants. There is a sickness in my soul which allows me no joy at my achievements. My possessions, my lovers, my power cause a kind of emotional nausea in me. I feel contempt for those I outplay, and contempt for myself. As I grow older, my longing for the temple becomes stronger day by day.*

*One night I dream of the incarnation of the Mother. I decide to leave everything behind me and return to the*

## Childhood, Healing and Humility

*temple to ask in humility if I can work my way up from the bottom once again.*

*As I am clothing myself appropriately to return, I hear the news from a servant – the incarnation of the Mother has died.*

*Even now she has evaded me. The pain is unbearable. I run through the streets to the temple. It is a long way and I am no longer young but I do not think of asking for transport. I run up the steps and burst into the temple. Although I no longer have access to it, no-one attempts to stop me. I am possessed by my pain.*

*I rush with tears dripping from my chin to the great round hall where the Mother lies before the altar. Even the guards at the door make no attempt to stop me from entering. It is as if all normal rules have ceased to exist. I throw myself on my knees beside the body of the Mother. I plead for forgiveness. I moan my pain. I leave tears and snot on the precious cloth covering her. No-one intervenes. My despair that she has gone from me before I can speak to her consumes all my being. I feel my heart will burst, and I wish that it would.*

*The awareness of a presence makes me look up. The incarnation of the Mother is standing before me, just as her body is lying beside me. "Come back, child," she says "there is nothing to forgive." She touches me on my forehead, and I fall unconscious to the floor, seared through by light.*

## TIME AND TIME AGAIN

*For the remaining years of my life I do not speak. My hair turns white almost over night. From this day on I am given the freedom to come and go as I will in the temple and in the town. When the new incarnation of the Mother is elected and dedicates her life to this form of service, I am seated on her left. I never question why this has come to pass nor does anyone else. I am acknowledged as a kind of holy fool, and the ability to heal with my hands flows through me effortlessly.*

*Almost every day I sit on the wide steps leading up to the temple. There the poorest people come to be healed. I sit for many hours each day, the birds pecking busily around me, the children playing up and down the steps. I take one suffering person after another onto my lap and lay my hands upon them, and if they can be healed, they are. The light flows through me, and the ecstasy of the flow transforms me. There is no greater beauty than this.*

*About three years after my meeting with the spirit of the Mother, I die quietly on the steps.*

### Concluding Comments

The experience of this healing flow was so intense that I can invoke it in a second, by closing my eyes and "finding" myself again on those steps. What limits me now is my mind. It seems remarkable to me now, when I look back on that Atlantean life when I healed the poor on the steps, that in those days nothing in me

## Childhood, Healing and Humility

questioned my ability. I did not block it by looking for methods, seeking techniques, or doubting myself in cases where no recovery occurred. I simply and unquestioningly saw the divinity in every seeking human who came, loved them, and unconsciously worshipped them as expressions of the divine. If people resonated with this awareness, and it was in their highest interests, they healed.

Now it is harder to stop doubt from creeping in. I'm better at healing the mind and emotions, which can be given the label of "therapy", than at healing the body.

On the other hand, if disturbances are caught before they get too advanced, the body will follow the lead of the mind and emotions anyway. Some years ago, however, after I learned the skill of theta healing, I began to allow "miraculous" healings to happen again. Sometimes they do, sometimes they don't. It seems to depend on the willingness of the person to heal, on karmic elements, and also on my acceptance that I really can let the flow through. The advice of my expanded self was, do it – it's your birthright.

Healing seems to be a little like walking on water – thinking about it doesn't help. But there can be those beautiful moments when we think we are merely walking on earth, only to discover afterwards that divine grace has allowed us to cross the water.

## CHAPTER 2

## Scars of Persecution

Along with encouraging us to attend theosophical lectures, my parents took us to church sometimes, and also sent us to Sunday School if there was one handy. These tended to be Anglican or Presbyterian churches, depending on which was closer. Like so many other children, I expect, I remember listening to some minister talking about God, and thinking to myself, it's not right that he says that. He isn't really close to God. I could not understand why the grown ups took the ministers so seriously.

Something else I did not understand was why I used to faint in church when I was a teenager in Samoa. We lived there for four years, because my parents decided to experience the tropics, so my father applied for a position as a teacher at Samoa College. In spite of trying to fight against it, I used to faint during the Anglican church services there. The same thing almost happened in Wells cathedral only a few years ago although I was loving the service, which seemed to come from an expanded awareness. And again I nearly fainted in the Liberal Catholic church in Auckland.

It was nothing to do with the denomination, but the sight of the celebrants in their robes carrying the cross triggered the feeling that I had to leave the planet. I have never done an actual past life regression to the source of my tendency to faint in High Church contexts. But I do have memories of being tried by the Inquisition for heresy, and of their attempts to get me to recant on the rack. The sight of the clerics seems to touch the cellular memory of the trial.

This fear of proclaiming unorthodox views before the church came up again in this life when I was invited by the Lutheran Church in Germany to give a talk on reincarnation at a Lutheran conference in the year 2000 - surely a daring topic for them to have taken. Perhaps they hoped to make people supporting such views look foolish (although there are a number of places in the Bible which express the belief that a person has reincarnated). Perhaps they were simply very progressive. In any case, I was invited to speak.

Although I had every reason not to go, as I was co-leading another seminar that weekend, I felt compelled to re-arrange my responsibilities so that I could talk to the Lutherans. I had felt such blank terror at the idea of standing up before them and expounding theories which were not part of current church dogma that I realized I had to give the talk no matter how complicated it would make my life. I recognized it as an opportunity to update my inner software about "heresy".

I gave the talk, was not tortured as my body seemed to expect, and came away a little freer. Unfortunately I had to rush back to my other seminar immediately after the talk, so I could not be sure what effect my words had had. However as I left the building people crowded around me eager to ask more questions.

There are numerous fears associated with using spiritual and healing gifts. Our bodies hold ancient cellular memories of persecution, which no longer serve us. It is time to come out with our abilities and skills - hiding them away because of old fears is pointless, but very common. Usually the fears are not conscious, but they result in people holding back unnecessarily. This is one of the areas in which past life work can be most useful.

I remember vividly the first seminar I gave to teach people past life work. It was attended by six people, four of whom were psychologists.

The intention was to meet one evening a week in Wiesenbach, near Heidelberg. On the first evening, after explaining the theory behind past life work, I wanted to demonstrate a regression with a volunteer from among the participants so that the others could see how to accompany someone in past life work. After that, they were to work in pairs with each other. I thought I would take a "safe" theme for that first demonstration regression, so I chose the topic "The life in which you felt most connected to God".

The volunteer for that regression was a pretty, plumpish young woman with soft blonde curls, and a winning manner. She seemed out-going, friendly and confident. She was a registered nurse, and was considering free lance work. I could see no reason why I should not do the demonstration regression with her.

You can imagine the horror on the participants' faces and my own consternation, when she started screaming terribly as soon as she entered the other life. She was re-experiencing having her hands cut off. She had stepped into a life in which she had indeed felt extremely closely connected to God, in fact she had felt so connected that she had been a very successful healer, well known for her skill. She had become so well-known that the local ruler had called her to heal his son, who was desperately ill. She had been unable to save the boy, and as "punishment" the ruler had had her hands cut off. Logically enough, she had been reticent about using her healing skills in her current life. After the regression, she could see that her fear of being seen as a healer was now inappropriate. She felt free to come out again with her abilities.

And I realized there are no "safe" topics.

## TIME AND TIME AGAIN

It is not so usual to step straight into the worst crisis in the life being reviewed. It is more common for a client to enter the past life in early adulthood, and to approach the main issues gradually.

The following is another example from my own life of becoming aware of unconscious, emotionally charged, limiting memories, but this time it happened spontaneously.

I lived for twelve years with my children in Neckargemuend, a village near Heidelberg in Germany. In that area people would celebrate the start of Spring with a parade. They carried decorated sticks threaded with boiled eggs and pretzels, a band played traditional summer songs, and the local children dressed up as ladybugs and butterflies. The focal point of the procession was a cart with an effigy of a snowman on it. At the end of the parade everyone assembled on a field, and the snowman was burnt, symbolically declaring the end of winter.

I had managed to avoid the burning part of this ceremony for several years, but when my daughter was in kindergarten, she wanted to watch it with her friends. As the wood for the bonfire was stacked up, I could feel myself becoming increasingly agitated. The urge to run away was almost uncontrollable, and I was struggling not to faint. But I had a four year old to care for, and no-one nearby could possibly understand what was happening for me.

## Scars of Persecution

I did my best to breath slowly and focus on other things. As the snowman effigy was tied to a pole in the middle of the pile of firewood and the fire was lit to cheers and laughter from the crowd, it was almost more than I could bear. The smoke blew towards me. And I remembered.

### *Past Life Experience*

*I am a child of about nine, a girl. I am dressed in a pinafore over another dress and my long, dark hair, a bit greasy, is in plaits which are tied back. The setting seems to be England in the middle ages. There are half-timbered houses surrounding a square. I am being held at an open window overlooking the square so I can't run away, and I'm being forced to look out. Strong hard arms hold me so tightly it hurts, and I can feel the breasts of this woman pushing into my back. She smells sour.*

*In the centre of the square is a huge pile of firewood piled around a central post. A cart has been drawn up, and in it is my mother. I didn't recognize her at first. Her hair has been cut off and little bits stick up in irregular chunks. Her head looks scratched. She is dirty and ragged, and seems barely able to stand. What have they done to her?*

*The grip on my arms tightens. "This is what happens to people who work with the devil," hisses the voice of my captor. "Learn from her sins and be saved." The woman imprisoning me in her arms is the priest's housekeeper. Her hands are rough, and she has a pinched, mean face with dark eyes and reddened cheeks. The priest doesn't have a wife. When the men came some days ago and dragged my mother away, I ran across the paddocks to the home of a neighbour. But the priest sent this woman to get me.*

*The priest is down there saying something, but there is a roaring in my ears. A man ties my mother to the pole.*

*I call out to her, but my voice sounds strange and cracked. Only a small movement indicates that she may have heard. A murmuring sound comes from the crowd as the man lights the fire. Then there is only noise like a terrible storm. I start to fight and scream, and I bite the arms holding me. The woman whacks me. The fire is growing, the storm in my head is getting louder and louder. I faint.*

*I don't remember much about that life. I am forced to work in the priest's house, and abused daily by him and his housekeeper. My emotions gradually die, so that I seem petrified and retarded. At 15 or 16 I run away, take up with destitute people, and die young of illness and a broken spirit.*

*My beautiful mother was a herbalist and midwife, but the church did not approve of her methods. I was born out of wedlock, so was considered a child of sin. My mother did not believe in the teachings of the church, which said we were condemned to eternal damnation. She said all living things were children of God.*

*And she was right too. As I leave my body in that painful life she is there in spirit to take me to the light. She is as beautiful and radiant as I remember her in life, and her love carries me to the realms of truth and beauty.*

## Concluding Comments

When I asked myself in the expanded state after my death in that life, why I had chosen those very difficult experiences, it became clear that it was to experience that love and truth persist through all adversity. I also needed to know that truth is stronger than dogma, and love stronger than hate.

The message of my "then" self to my current self, was to live my mother's wisdom, and let go of the hesitation about revealing my true nature. Yet sometimes the body is reactivated in its old fear, even though the spirit knows better. This is all part of letting go of the ego, of the limiting stories we tell ourselves, and becoming free. Such emotionally charged experiences can take a long time to dissipate, however, even when they have been brought into conscious awareness.

I did not faint that day in the fields when they burnt the snowman. I disciplined myself to look at the children,

# TIME AND TIME AGAIN

to observe the leaves, to breathe deeply, to listen to the voices. Yes, life does go on. We can let the waves of emotion go.

If you are contemplating doing past life work, it's a comfort to know that we tend to call up the most painful lives first - these are the ones that are most impacting on us in our present life. The decisions that we made with a high emotional charge to them are those that are most vividly encoded when we incarnate again. This is why spontaneously remembered former lives, and those looked at during regressions, tend to be dramatic. I have never heard of anyone taking as the theme for a regression "the most harmless and mediocre life I have ever lived", though probably they will have lived countless simple lives too.

Perhaps one of the virtues of the realism of many movies is that it allows us to "re-experience" some of the more difficult fates we have lived through in the distant past without the need to do a regression, thus allowing our emotional bodies to gradually let go of some of the stored horror. Certainly some of the better directors must have vivid subconscious memories of historical situations to be able to portray them so truthfully. I think most viewers can tell at once which portrayals are authentic and which are just reconstructed fakes.

# CHAPTER 3

## Inner and Outer Space

Fear of persecution was not the only habitual emotion I had brought to earth with me this time round. The desire to pray was inherent in me too. As a child, I prayed fervently and frequently, seeming to have the belief, which no-one had told me to have in this life, that you had to kneel in order to pray.

I was a slender, big-eyed child with straight hair, which I would have loved to be curly. My mother did not believe in children being conceited, so I was convinced that I was thin and plain. Every evening after my mother said good night and turned out the light, I would wait till my sister had gone to sleep, then climb out of bed, kneel beside it, and pray. I prayed for everything imaginable, including the Queen of England! I was always afraid that my mother, who was usually very understanding, would come back into the room and find me out of bed and be angry with me. But she never found out about my praying

# TIME AND TIME AGAIN

One day during interval at school, a fat girl rushed up to me gasping "Come quick. Your sister's split her head open. She's in the staff room." Feeling faint, my own head like a dark vacuum, I pushed my way into the staff room without knocking, the fat girl peering excitedly past my shoulder, keen to have a sensational story to relate. My sister was sitting on the staff-room table looking pale. The headmaster stood beside her looking bemusedly at a large bloody wad of cotton wool with hair stuck to it. Apparently my sister had fallen from some banisters onto concrete steps and cut her head. It wasn't really such a big cut, but it got infected and my sister became quite ill. There was some talk that she might have tetanus.

I was about 10 years old, and I felt the need to pray for her. As I was still convinced I had to kneel to pray, I didn't know how to do this in the classroom. So several times a day I got permission from the teacher to go to the toilet. I'm sure Mr Collins must have wondered about my sudden need to leave the room so frequently, but he didn't say anything.

As soon as I got out of the classroom, I would slip behind the large entrance doors to the school, which were clipped open creating a hidden space behind them. Fearing all the time that someone would find me there and think I was stealing from the schoolbags, which we left in the corridor, I would kneel behind the doors and pray for my sister, or I went down to the toilet shed. The toilets in those days were stinky long-

## Inner and Outer Space

drops, but I knelt on the floor and prayed for my sister nevertheless. She got better, thank goodness, and no-one discovered my deception. It was a relief to discover later that I could pray anywhere and didn't have to kneel.

A place which filled me with a wave of mystical ecstasy similar to that of praying, though purer as it carried no burden of intention, was the fern house at the botanical gardens. Our parents took us to the gardens sometimes for picnics, and I would run on ahead as fast as I could to get to the fern house first. I wanted to be there alone to feel the peaceful presence of the fern spirits before anyone else came in and disturbed them. Being in the bush had a similar effect, but we were not often there. The tendency to move into a state of ecstatic oneness when I am alone in undisturbed nature has always been with me. If it occasionally does not happen when I'm in a forest, on a lonely beach, or in the bush, I feel almost cheated.

When I was 24 and studying in Heidelberg, I had an experience which changed the foundation of my life forever. I had experienced a completely normal day. It was not even a phase in my life when I was meditating a lot or reading spiritual books. Nor was I going through an emotional upheaval at the time. I had been in the English Department of Heidelberg University, in the library, had worked in the student cafeteria in the lunch break, and then after dark taken the rattly old tram home to my room in a suburb of Heidelberg called

# TIME AND TIME AGAIN

Eppelheim. I got ready for bed as usual, and had just put out the light to get into bed, when I was struck by a wave of such overwhelming and tangible love that I thought someone visible to the human eye must be emitting it. Although almost unable to stand through its power, I put the light back on again, feeling I must then be able to see the source of the outpouring. To my physical eyes there was nothing to see, but the flood of love caught me up and I lost consciousness and fell onto the bed.

Next morning when I awoke, everything had changed. It was as if a river of pristine clarity was flowing between me and the world, allowing me to see everything as it really is. Or to put it another way, as if a dimming veil had been removed between me and the world. There was nothing anywhere which was not beautiful. I saw the same beauty in dirt, cars and buildings as in flowers, trees and people. I was overwhelmed and weak-kneed at the glory and simplicity of all phenomena.

Bathed in this new awareness, I went about life as if nothing had happened, although I sometimes had to sit down when the strength of the vision became too exquisite to bear. I had no idea whether this state of being would go on for the rest of my life, no idea what would happen. I had no-one to confide in or to seek guidance from.

## Inner and Outer Space

It was the time of the Vietnam War, and I had been an ardent protester against the horrors that were part of that war. In this state of new seeing-ness, however, I discovered that when I focussed on the war, everything in it seemed infinitely beautiful, meaningful, and filled with love. It was as if the Divine was saying "This too is part if my wholeness." There seemed to be nothing but limitless, compassionate acceptance, as if everything that was happening was part of the expression of those individuals, not judged, not rejected, not praised, yet fully seen.

The intensity of this new awareness lasted continuously for three days, and then gradually began to fade, coming and going in waves for another few weeks. Although I have not retained its insight as a constant state of being, it gave me a basic awareness which is present under all the illusions and fears that my ego still conjures up.

All these experiences seemed to lead automatically to my interest in past lives.

Also, I had briefly died immediately after my birth, perhaps keeping the veil between the worlds more penetrable than it is for most people. Through my upbringing as a theosophist, I had heard about reincarnation from an early age, and accepted the idea as "normal". Many of my own inner tendencies seem to have their origins in past lives. A further experience which was also unsought but had a definite past life reference occurred in the midst of a seminar I was co-leading in Bonn.

For seven years, together with several co-trainers, I led "The Sage Experience" in the main cities in Germany. It is a very intense weekend seminar which forms an excellent basis for life and spiritual growth. It is normally led by two to four trainers, supported by a large team of assistants. One of the people who often assisted was a young man who, to our great distress, developed a huge tumour. It had grown into his lungs and heart, so was inoperable. He went through all the horrors of chemotherapy and radiation, and was frequently on the brink of death. In spite of his fragile state, he had signed up to be an assistant for this "Sage Experience" in Bonn. Dragging himself around, he seemed on the very cusp of death.

After completing the Saturday part of the seminar by about 11 o'clock in the evening, the participants left to sleep. The assistant team formed a circle with the trainers to bond and share before the final day of the seminar. In that circle my co-leader suggested that we do a healing ritual for the young man with the tumour. As my colleague glanced at me his eyes held the question whether he or I should lead the ritual. I indicated with a head movement that he should go ahead – some vague, barely conscious sense of inadequacy held me back. We did the simple, brief, ritual, (and incidentally it seemed to be a turning point for the young man - he has meantime recovered completely), but as it progressed, a sense of terrible betrayal on my part began to fill me.

As the trainers adjourned to the trainer room, I could no longer contain the sobs, no longer could I be a mature, responsible seminar leader. I was shaken with a grief so deep it felt as if my body would crack into pieces and fall to the floor. Pictures began crossing my mind of other times when I could have healed, but hadn't. I saw a sailing ship approaching a wharf, the people on deck pleading that help be given to those sick with smallpox on board. They needed food, and medical care. I saw myself as a town official refusing the ship the right to dock although I had skills as a healer. I believed I had to prevent any contact, to avoid the spread of the illness to the town, but the eyes of the dying on the deck pierced me, and I knew my place should have been on board with them. The ship was forced to turn about, with death as the only outcome.

Pictures also came of Atlantis, or some similar civilization, where my co-leader and I would have been able to lessen the destruction if we had only worked with the huge crystals in the hills behind the town, instead of seeking our own safety. The enormity of my guilt seemed boundless, insurmountable, crushing; my remorse bottomless.

However, trainers must have the grit to push their own "stuff" aside for the duration of the seminar. Somehow, I remembered my role as a trainer that weekend and pulled myself together enough to head for the hotel room where my son, my daughter and I would spend the night. After my children were asleep and I lay in bed at last, I found myself no longer in my body. Or rather, I became aware that the atoms of my body had become the stars of the universe. There was little sense of my having any personal identity at all, but what there was of a "self" was streamed through with light in a never-ending outpouring. Some small remaining wisp of myself asked "Am I forgiven?" and received the awareness, "There is nothing to forgive".

I lay awake for the rest of the night in this state of universal formless, star-filled bliss, finding I was part of the universe and yet still had some slight awareness of personal individuality. I had no idea whether I still had a physical body, nor whether, supposing I still had one, I would be capable in the morning of moving it, or talking, or walking. None of that mattered. There was no sense of time.

I was interested to discover, however, when the alarm clock went off in the morning and my children struggled to wake up, that I could speak and I did still have a physical body. I could also move it with expertise, as if I had been doing that all my life. It was strange, in the awareness of my universal self, to watch and feel myself cleaning my teeth and getting dressed as if I had just spent a normal night sleeping.

## Inner and Outer Space

I returned to the last day of the seminar as if nothing had happened and did my work as a trainer as usual. Yet all the time in the background was this knowledge of myself as a presence in the universe, galaxies swirling within me. That expanded awareness came through my involuntary surrendering to the deepest darkness I had known. And awareness of that darkness came from past life memories.

## CHAPTER 4

## First Contact with Earth

Many dark experiences of the past show themselves to us in this life as physical problems. Past life work indicates that some chronically susceptible or painful parts of our current bodies may be expressing unresolved issues which have their origin in physical problems of previous lives. The former wounding or disease probably will not turn up in exactly the same way as before, but will often create "dis-ease" in the same area as in the former life. A gun-shot wound, for example, may appear as a birth mark, or unexplained dent, or as a tendency to have pain in a certain area of the body. A former drowning may show up as fear of water, but also as respiratory problems.

A huge number of us have, at some former time, experienced hanging or beheading. This can make us hesitant to speak up in situations which even remotely resemble the event which led to the execution, but can also make us susceptible to throat ailments.

## First Contact with Earth

In many cases, when in a state of trance, a person will feel they still have a spear or sword piercing some part of their body. Some of us can actually see this, and many of us can sense it. It needs to be removed from the energy body, and doing so can, in some cases, instantly bring relief from pain in the physical body.

One woman I worked with could not understand why she always felt pain in her foot when she attended one of my evening courses in spiritual development. She was a young mother, and it was always a great struggle for her to get the family meal done in time for the group, and then drag herself away from the children who wanted "Mummy to put us to bed" instead of Daddy. She normally arrived with a slightly bad conscience towards the family although it was her only night out each week, and she was very eager to participate.

We did a brief past life regression to the cause of the unexplained pain that occurred in her foot whenever she attended the group. Her foot did not trouble her at any other time. The story which arose was very telling. She (a man in that life) and her brother had been leaders of a group of nomadic tribesmen in the Middle East. They were in conflict with another group which was larger, and which had stolen animals from the brother's herds. The tribe conferred, and my client (in the male role she had then) wanted revenge on the other group and pleaded for a surprise attack on them. The brother and most of the rest of the family felt it was safer to swallow the loss and keep out of the larger groups way. Enraged by what he considered to be their cowardice, my client rode off with only a few followers and ambushed a group of men from the other tribe. In the ensuing fight, several of his supporters were killed, and he escaped with a severe axe wound in his foot. The wound became infected, and he died painfully of blood poisoning knowing that if he had listened to the advice of the family this would not have happened.

The connection to the client's present situation was clear - she was acting against the wishes of her family, and the cellular memory in her foot was activated, causing pain. The pain did not return after its origin had become conscious.

Another time, a middle-aged woman who had been operated on for a brain tumour came to me, as part of her healing process, wanting to investigate the life which held the origin for that tumour. She entered a life in the Middle Ages in which she had been kicked by a horse on exactly the place of the tumour, while in a state of intense turmoil with her partner. In this life she recognized her son as having been the partner from the former life. Part of her healing was to resolve the conflict she was experiencing with her son in this life.

It was fascinating for me to see the connection between past and present lives in the case of a man in his fifties who came to me to gain more understanding as to why he had been born an albino. Being an albino meant he had extremely weak eyesight, and skin which burnt immediately if exposed to sunlight. When he was a child, there were no advanced sun block products, which meant he was forced to stay inside a lot of the time. For this reason he could not participate in sports. Only as an adult had he been able to take up sports such as skiing owing to the great improvement in products to support his eyesight and protect his skin.

On entering the life which held the origin of his albinism, he found himself in the arena as a famous gladiator in Roman times. He had fought countless times, but through his mental and physical prowess had never been vanquished. On this day he was attached to a plinth to limit his movement and was warding off spears thrown at him. He was focused and efficient, sure of his ability. However, he miscalculated once and was struck in the eye by a spear, causing instant blindness.

Almost overnight he went from being an acclaimed fighter to being a blind beggar. Deep within him he resolved that he would never in all eternity develop physical prowess again; it was too dangerous. As the regression with my client progressed, we experienced his physical decay in that life through hunger and mistreatment. Many wanted to avenge themselves on him. Finally he was imprisoned in an underground cellar because he had stolen bread. It was there that he turned more and more into himself, seeking some meaning in the blows he had suffered in life. Shortly before his death, he had a vision of blinding light and the feeling of oneness with the Divine. This seemed to him the most important awareness in his life. He felt that it had made his life worth living.

In the realms between lives, in contact with his expanded self, he saw that he had chosen that life to experience the extreme juxtaposition of physical prowess and physical weakness, and that beyond them both there was a transcendent Truth. We saw how, through being an albino in his current life, he had radically avoided the possibility of being physically outstanding and the danger with which that seemed to be linked. And as the vision of light and oneness with God had occurred when he was blind, he had chosen weak sight as a link to his spirituality. He saw that now the time had come when he could experience both physical and spiritual strength without danger.

For me too, physical reactions in this life were often related to past life events. After my divorce and a severe illness, I had been confronted with panic attacks which were so extreme that for a year or so I collapsed fairly regularly and would be taken to hospital, only to be discharged some time later because nothing seriously wrong could be discovered. Although as time went on I became more skilful at dealing with the attacks so that I could usually avoid collapsing, the panic was very distressing to me, as it was always accompanied by the feeling that I was dying and nobody could help me. I felt that doctors or other kind and qualified people were incapable of treating me appropriately, as they had no experience of what to do with "people like me". In this regression I asked to re-experience the life which held the origin of my panic attacks.

## *Past Life Experience*

*The spaceship I am travelling in has landed in an area which feels like the highlands of Scotland. I look out onto stony, heather-covered ground and see that we are on a plateau on the side of a slope. It is a small craft, and only three of us are on board. We had set off from our vast mother ship in this little vehicle to do a brief reconnoitre and collect samples of earth matter. We are from the Pleiades. I have decided to be one of those whose task is to seed a higher consciousness on Earth, and I want to take a first close look at the blue-green planet. I am extremely curious, and full of loving expectation.*

*The other two are here to collect samples of plant growth and minerals to take back to the mother-ship so we can better understand the way things work in this dense, slow sort of matter. The others are in a different part of the project than I am, and they have gone to collect specimens, leaving me to mind the ship. I can call them from the instrument panel if anything unexpected happens but I have been asked not to leave the ship till they get back.*

*We are slender, slightly transparent beings, with a shape similar to that of humans, only considerably taller. We radiate a golden light, which changes tone depending on our feelings. We have a defined form, but are of energy rather than matter. We can merge without resistance with others of our kind if both desire to do so, and this is a wonderful way to share love and extend our personal range of experience. Each takes on the stored experience fields of the other, which enriches both. There is no differentiation into male and female. I can merge with anyone who shares this wish with me. The strongest energy centre in our bodies shines with a pinkish hue and is somewhat higher in the body than the human heart centre.*

*I have become aware of a subtle change in my body since being on Earth. It seems to have become denser, a bit more solid, so that I feel as if I am contained by a very fine membrane. I wonder if that impression will go when we take off again.*

*As far as I know I have always had this body through all the aeons of my existence. It is not separate from my essence. If we become tired as an individual, we can merge into energy balancing with others for a while, which redistributes our energies, and we re-emerge regenerated.*

## First Contact with Earth

*Time passes slowly as I wait for the other two to return. I am not used to feeling the passage of time. In other dimensions we seldom think in terms of time, we just are. The others are gone much longer than I had expected, and I feel an unfamiliar nervousness. I am consumed with curiosity to set my feet on this strange new world. Surely it wouldn't matter if I went out and kept within sight of the ship. I step down onto the hard stony ground and feel the clear, strong, very tangible air around me. This is Earth! How solid and how beautiful! How strong and clear cut! How surging with energy! I touch the stiff, prickly texture of the heather plants and the sharp edges of the stones. I feel strong and radiant as I am stroked by the wind. The air is amazingly "thick" compared to any I have known before, and it is laden with new and intriguing odours. It is almost like walking through vibrant, airy jelly. Flying creatures row and soar their way through it and give clear and exciting cries, which set the air vibrating.*

*As I move across the stony ground, I am intoxicated by the new sensations I experience. The wind brushing across my "skin" makes me feel I am burning along the edges of my energy body as I move on along a track, fascinated by this world I have chosen to work in.*

*Then I see my first humans. I'm shocked and fascinated. They look even stranger than I had been led to believe. There is a group of them further down the slope. They are short and very hairy, and they have hairy garments hung over them. Their eyes look at the surface rather than within, and they seem very agitated at seeing me. To my eyes they seem, forgive me, very ugly, and even at this distance they smell bad, very bad. I really can feel, in my state of rather naive righteousness, that they need my refining influence. I feel a wave of love for these strange hairy beings with whom I will soon be working, and feel sure they will be pleased to join energy with me so that they need no longer feel fear. I radiate love down to them, and open my arms in an embracing gesture as I move a step or two towards them.*

*But what is this? They grunt and make angry gestures. I can feel that I've frightened them. I send another wave of love towards them, and ignoring the smell, take another step. Then one takes up a stone and hurls it at me. The stone tears the membrane of my body causing terrible pain.*

*Never before have I experienced an attack on my body. Never before in all the millennia of my existence has my body been violated. The pain and shock is indescribable. They are trying to destroy me, which for me means all of my being. I have no awareness that on Earth a "soul" can separate from a body, that the body is not also the soul. I do not know that the life force can retire from the body and enter another one at a later time. Soul and body were always one to me - one, eternal, and constantly in a state of regeneration. This searing pain as more stones hit me is as shattering as*

## First Contact with Earth

*the realization that another life form wishes to harm me - wishes to harm me without knowledge of my intentions. Never has violence been part of my experience, and this violence is unfounded. I send out waves of desperate pleas for help, but there is no reaction. Not one of my people is there to help me.*

*The rocks thud and crush. Terror and pain overwhelm me. My body sinks down into a blob of jelly. Life is in it no longer.*

*It is not until a period of bottomless darkness and despair has passed that my consciousness can be reached by the light beings that guide us after death. I am gradually nursed out of shock by the light beings and realize that my life force, my individuality, still exists even without my body. My cycle of lives on Earth has begun.*

*As I was dying, I formed the conviction that you can only live on Earth if you look like the others and have a body of flesh and blood. This is what I then manifested in my first real Earth life. In it I was a Stone Age man. In that life, the cave in which I sheltered with my partner, my two small children and some others collapsed in an earthquake. My partner was crushed. I got the children outside, but was struck by a huge, falling rock which broke my backbone so that I could no longer move. I bled to death, paralysed, knowing my children would be devoured by the next marauding beast, as they were too small to defend themselves. My conviction while dying that time, was that even in a physical body, life on Earth cannot be trusted.*

*I had dived in at the deep end of earthly experience, as it were, of getting to know that life in the material world of duality is a great challenge. It was going to take a while before I could accept that Heaven can also be on Earth.*

## Concluding Comments

This first death as a space being made a deeper impression on me than most of the following ones. In the deaths that followed I knew at some level that my soul would continue to live after the body was laid aside. In that first death I was not aware of this. It took several re-visits to the event and a deep expression of my horror and loss before I was able to view the events with some degree of equanimity. I had to learn to accept that I had chosen to learn of duality in this extreme way. But the experience runs very deep. Watching the film "Powder" some years later called up all the old desolation, and left me feeling inconsolable. It's a film where an "alien" in human form struggles to be accepted on Earth and finally manages to leave it.

My excessive fear did abate after this regression however, and I realized that my struggle with anxiety has been a prime motivator on my path of spiritual growth, so in this respect it has served the greater good.

## First Contact with Earth

While in the space between lives after my death as the Pleiadian visitor, I looked at the reason for these experiences. I saw that I had chosen to move into the challenges of life on Earth as deeply and thoroughly as possible. How else could I comprehend the beings I was working with if I had not understood what they would be called upon to confront?

# CHAPTER 5

## Relationships and Jealousy

Understanding relationships is another one of the challenges on Earth.

My relationship with Rainer, the father of my daughter, needed all the help it could get. And as the time we were together was right in the middle of my training in past life work, it was to past life work that I turned to try to sort out our difficulties.

Rainer was a tall, bearded man, with warm brown eyes. He had already been married once, and had two daughters who lived with their mother. Judging from his enjoyment of cycling and kicking a ball about, he would have been a good sportsman, but a sedentary job as a teacher and then trainer in superlearning had left him a little overweight. He had been a passionate and innovative teacher, and when I got to know him had just left his school teaching career to set up an institute for "Suggestopedia", a form of accelerated learning, pioneered by Dr Georgi Losanov in Bulgaria.

## Relationships and Jealousy

The six years we were in partnership were strenuous in spite of our good intentions. The original delight I felt at being invited away for a weekend with a man I admired, a man introducing accelerated learning into the staid German education system, a man with a deep, melodious voice and the demeanour of a leader faded. Still, I was filled with the joy of a new relationship after my divorce from the boys' father, and I was eager for us to live together.

Mind you, it must have been quite a hurdle for him to move in with me and two sons. And it took him three months after our decision to cohabit before he actually took the plunge and joined us, although we had been mutually renting a house all that time. During the five years we lived together, he moved out several times, only to return again at intervals.

He could not tolerate my "high energy" as he called it. He could not sleep in the same bed as me, but retired after sex to his own bed, leaving me feeling undesirable. He liked women with "big bums and tits", neither of which I sported.

So here we were after a few years together, deciding to separate, but slipping into bed again for one last cuddle.

Six weeks after that last cuddle there was no evading the fact that I was pregnant. That one last cuddle had done the trick in spite of contraception. As my period stubbornly stayed away day after day, I resorted to asking my pendulum if I was pregnant. "No" it obligingly replied day after day, just as I willed it to. But even the pendulum had to admit defeat and change direction after a couple more weeks. I could not believe it – 43 and pregnant, just when the boys, aged 14 and 10, were getting a lot more independent. Rainer and I decided to stay together after all, because of the baby. An abortion was not something I could have gone ahead with, so I refused to listen to any statistics about handicapped babies born to women over 40, and after crying for two days at the loss of my freedom, I knuckled down to make my body a suitable temple for the coming new life, and to greet that new life with as much joy as possible.

My boys were curious and positive about the thought of having a baby brother or sister. The older of the two had recently come to live with me after spending some years with his father following our divorce. The separation had been a hard and horrible time for all of us, and I was so happy to have my beautiful elder son living with me again. His formerly blond curls were darkening but his enormous blue eyes with dark lashes were as striking as they had been when he was a toddler. Old ladies used to buy him chocolate in shops they were so charmed by his angelic looks. I didn't believe in giving children sweets so I used to intervene.

His younger brother had brown eyes like me, and was a brilliant artist from the age of three. I organised his first exhibition when he was only seven. He loved nature

## Relationships and Jealousy

passionately in any of its forms, wanting to take earthworms into his bath with him, and filling his pockets with slugs. But now both boys were growing up, and gradually the elder one was treating his younger brother with a little more affection. In their younger years he had done his best to make his little brother's life miserable, but the little brother had stoically adored him in spite of it.

A blow came in the fourth month of the new pregnancy when I began getting strong contractions far too early. The doctor decided he would have to sew my cervix shut to prevent a premature birth. This was standard practice in Germany at the time, but it had to be done just at a time when Rainer had booked to go to Greece by himself for a ten day holiday. I expected he would cancel his holiday to support me through the hospital ordeal, but he did not.

On his return from Greece, he said he had met a woman there who felt attracted to him. Her name was Hildegard and she lived in Cologne. A week or two later, to my distress, she came to Neckargemuend, where we lived, and spent a day with us. She was intelligent, efficient, pleasant enough to look at in a slightly boring, "good-girl" way, but certainly not stunning. However she was singularly focussed on her goal to take over Rainer.

I was obviously pregnant, and Rainer and I were living together. I expected that this would show her that she should keep out of our lives. It didn't, and she made no attempt to hide her desire. I was deeply hurt, and felt even worse when Rainer visited her on his trips through Germany giving seminars. "Why aren't you happy for me?" he would ask. Do you think women ever are happy when their partner is in an intense relationship with some other woman?

Rainer was with me for the birth of our daughter, and travelled to New Zealand with me and the children when our daughter was two months old. After our return, however, when she was six months old, he went to visit Hildegard in Cologne. Our baby daughter had measles at the time, and was ill with a high fever. I felt oppressed and worried about her illness and I was exhausted by taking care of her day and night. Rainer did not come back that night, and I learnt later that he and Hildegard had slept together.

I was painfully jealous, and this became no easier when Hildegard decided to move to Neckargemuend so as to be near Rainer. He even offered her a job in his institute.

To me such behaviour was incomprehensibly cruel. Jealousy ate its way like an evil green worm in my guts. With all the spiritual training I had done, I was conscious enough to realize that this ought to be a chance for inner growth, and that I could aim at practising unconditional love, and non-attachment, but

## Relationships and Jealousy

I loathed Hildegard and felt physically sick with jealousy.

On endless walks I tried to lift my spirit. I prayed, I tried to forgive, I used all the spiritual techniques I could think of in an attempt to quench the sickening power the jealousy had over me, but it still held sway. It seemed as if my connection to this woman went far deeper than could be explained by the chance happenings of this life. So at the first opportunity, in the desperate hope of finding relief, I did the following past life regression to the source of our karmic connection.

### *Past Life Experience*

*I enter the regression as Mother Superior of a convent in Spain in the 14th century. It is early evening and still light, but the outside doors of the convent are already closed for the night, and I have retired to my rooms to attend to business and to contemplate. To my irritation a nun knocks nervously at my door and, obviously apprehensive of my reaction, tells me that my cousin is outside and is demanding to see me. Hoping to be rid of my relative quickly, I do not ask that she be brought to me, but walk grimly, with clattering rosary, to the little gridded window in the massive main door. I throw open the shutter and ask sharply what the matter is.*

# TIME AND TIME AGAIN

*My cousin's face is smeared with tears, and she looks as if she is pregnant again. She is holding a grubby baby in her arms and a toddler is clinging to her skirts. It has snot running down into its mouth, and has obviously been crying, although now it just stares at me with its mouth open.*

*When she sees me, my cousin bursts into tears again. She says that her husband has been caught poaching on the land of the local baron, and is to be executed the next day. She begs me to intervene on her behalf.*

*I am irritated by this show of excessive emotion, by the unkemptness of my relatives, and by her so obvious fertility. "I cannot intervene in worldly matters," I snap, although the baron respects the church and might actually listen to me. "You would do well to pray." I slam the shutter closed again, and stalk back to my rooms. But my peace of mind has gone, and my conscience begins to prick me. As darkness falls my agitation increases. Must I not show compassion? What will become of those children? Mother of Mercy be with me. Immaculate Mother guide me.*

*I rise while it is still dark, request that my mule be made ready, and set off towards the baron's castle with a small entourage. As we approach the castle the sky is just beginning to show the first suggestion of light although the stars are still visible. We are moving along beside the castle walls and the sky is turning pink when we notice a straggling group of people coming towards us pushing a barrow. As they come closer I see my cousin. Her husband's body lies in the barrow. He has just been hanged.*

*As she comes up to me she screams abuse. "May God curse you in all eternity for your arrogance!" are the words that strike home most.*

*Back at the convent I repent that I had waited before going to the baron. I do penance and go on a pilgrimage. I decide that the convent should serve the community more, and open some rooms to be used as a refuge for the sick and wounded. In those troubled times, we have plenty to do tending them. I often work side by side with the sisters.*

*Although I never fully forgive myself, I die a pleasant death in this life, surrounded by praying nuns, with the sweet tones of others singing at a distance. At the time of my death most people consider me a great benefactress of the community.*

## Concluding Comments

Of course my cousin who lost her husband in this regression was the being who became Rainer's lover in my current life. I feel that much of my agitation towards Hildegard was caused by the deep-seated memory of her curse, and my related sub-conscious feeling of guilt.

# TIME AND TIME AGAIN

From a higher perspective I could acknowledge that it was somehow appropriate that she should have "taken" my partner in this life just as I had "taken" hers (or at least not saved him) previously, both of us being left with children.

Some years later, after Rainer and I had separated, I accidentally re-met Hildegard. To my surprise, as she approached me, tears came into her eyes and she said, "If I have caused you pain, I ask for forgiveness." I embraced her silently, and have not seen her since, but there has been a definite shift in the energy between us. Although I still feel unable to understand on a human level why Hildegard acted the way she did in this life, I no longer hold any grudge towards her. There is a sense of balance.

On another level I can also see how the death of her husband in that life, and my resulting bad conscience, served the community. Through my attempts in that life to "make it up to God" by caring for the sick and wounded, numerous other lives were saved. Sometimes the deeds of individuals can have meaning in a greater framework than we realize.

## CHAPTER 6

## The Gift of Unconditional Love

So now it is time to introduce Bernd.

Bernd seems almost the opposite of Rainer. Whereas Rainer was barrel-chested and had a tendency to be overweight, Bernd was extremely tall and thin. Rainer had brown eyes, very tanned skin and a beard; Bernd was blond, clean-shaven and blue-eyed. Rainer was five years older than me, and was dignified to the verge of seeming a little pompous if he didn't feel at home somewhere. Bernd was fourteen years younger than me, boyish and shy.

I had met him on my first visit to a spiritual community some time after Rainer and I had started living together. At that time, Bernd had just returned to the centre after a long overland pilgrimage to connect with Sai Baba. He seemed to me the epitome of a spiritual seeker who would put God before anything else. For me it was wonderful to feel close to someone that I could be open with about my spiritual experiences, and who was interested in my desire to take a spiritual path. With all previous boyfriends I had tried to hide this longing in myself, as it seemed clear they would not understand it. I was impressed by Bernd's dedication to a spiritual life.

Sometimes, while I was supposed to be doing the cleaning at the centre, he showed me little films of his time with Sai Baba. These were a welcome relief from the work, and I enjoyed his company.

So you can imagine how amazed and touched I felt when, shortly after my return from the spiritual community, he rang, and suggested he might visit us. I was living with Rainer and my sons, but I felt very attracted to Bernd. We had spent quite a lot of time together at the centre, but had not had any romantic closeness, apart from a rather long hug as I left. He knew I lived with another man, and it was clear to both of us that if he came, we would respect Rainer and not have an affair. I do not think Bernd even wanted one. It would have meant too much responsibility. He needed the option of disappearing and living his own life when he wanted to.

I remember arranging for the older children to be off playing with friends when Bernd arrived, so we would have a chance to talk openly about what this weird sort of friendship might be. But then I got so agitated about his coming that I could not even drive to the station to pick him up. I thought we would just go on being comrades, but he held my hand after his arrival and it made my heart race and my face flush. How was this wonderful but complicating factor going to fit into my not very steady household? Bernd seemed filled with his own sense of innocence, and quite convinced that there was no reason why his stay should be inappropriate.

He was a wonderful support. He worked steadily in the house, did the shopping, mended things that had been broken for ages, in fact did all those odds and ends that Rainer never had time for. I had never felt so "seen" and appreciated in my life. No wonder Bernd became very dear to me, although we had no sexual contact.

Rainer was very jealous, but as long as Bernd and I were not jumping into bed behind his back, I felt innocent about our friendship. So when Rainer was away on that trip to Greece during my pregnancy, it was Bernd who came to take care of me after I got out of hospital. (Rainer knew about this). And after my daughter's birth, when Rainer had to go off to give seminars in the north of Germany and I got ill with mastitis and scarlet fever, it was again Bernd who hurried to my side.

Apart from my children, I had no relatives anywhere in Europe, and Bernd was like a particularly loving big brother, with just a hint of a romantic overtone. It was through Bernd that I had the possibility of starting to do past life regressions during the time of my daughter's babyhood, while I was so plagued by jealousy. He came and minded her when she was asleep in the mornings, so I could go to a nearby reincarnation therapist to do the regressions. This was before I trained in the method myself.

I can well remember my nervousness before my first regression. I had gone to a neat terraced house in a newly built suburb of Neckargemuend. It didn't look remotely "alternative", and nor did Benita von Kettler, who was going to accompany me into the past life. When she opened the door, I thought she looked like a well brought up middle-class mother, complete with a string of pearls and a pastel twin-set. We went into her living room, where she explained the method and we talked over what theme I should take. Once again, my burden of jealousy seemed my most dominant source of suffering, so we decided to take "the life which holds the origin of my jealousy" as the theme. Benita then asked me to lie down on the couch. She dimmed the room and started the relaxation phase. This is what came up.

### *Past Life Experience*

*As I enter this life I can not even make out whether I am a man or a woman. I am simply aware of deadly cold. I am plodding through snow, and I am leading a pony. It is not until I feel the icicles from my condensed*

## The Gift of Unconditional Love

*breath hanging from my moustache that I am sure that I am a man. It is quite a long thin moustache that hangs down on both sides of my mouth. I am about thirty, and the plain that I am struggling across is in Mongolia. There is only one thought in me - I must get back to my home; there is a woman waiting for me, but I do not even know if she will be there.*

*I am married to this woman, and I have left her. I now know that it was not right to have left her, and my one desire is to return in case she is still there.*

*It is the 17th century. I have been married to this woman for three years, and we were happy together in a quiet way, although we have had no children so far. Then travelling performers came to town, and with them was a woman who fascinated me. She came from India, and she had wavy hair, quite different from our straight-haired women, and she wore tinkling golden earrings. Her eyes were a rounder shape than ours, and her clothes showed her figure and a strip of skin around her waist. Our women did not show their skin. To me she embodied a kind of sensuality I had never experienced before, and she flirted with me with her flashing eyes. I could play a zither-like instrument well, and sing, and in the evenings I often went to their camp. So when her troupe moved on to the next town, I simply went with them on my pony. I did not even explain my actions to my wife.*

# TIME AND TIME AGAIN

*I stayed with the group till winter came, but it was clear that the Indian woman did not want me except as a passing conquest, nor was I drawn to her now that my curiosity was satisfied. There was no peace with this woman, and there were scenes of jealousy and foolishness with her group. It was clear that I would have to leave.*

*This was easier said than done, however. We had crossed the great plain in stages with the show, but now winter had come and the plain was deserted, a desert of ice and snow. Just before the first heavy snows fell, we had repeatedly heard the news that war had broken out in the region of my home town. The reports that filtered through suggested that it was worse than we had supposed at first. Apparently many people were on the run as refugees, trying to keep away from the fighting. The situation was evidently very chaotic, and now winter was there.*

*I thought of my wife. I had deserted her, and she would need me now. The extent of my irresponsibility became devastatingly clear to me, and a deep, bitter shame dragged me down. I began to long for her, for her quiet, strong presence, for her steadfastness. Where was she now, with war and winter surrounding her? I knew now, when it might be too late, that I loved her and must return to her.*

*But it was early winter, and the great plain of snow and ice lay between us. People said it was impossible to cross the great plain alone at this time of year. But I knew I must do it. It seemed like the only way to redeem myself for my cruelty. And I had to know if she was alive - I had to know if she was still at our home. I had to know.*

*I packed my pony and set off. At first I rode, but the going through the snow was hard work for the pony, so I walked, leading him. At night I dozed against his body, kept alive by his warmth. But by the fourth day it was clear that he was not going to survive. He did not want to eat the little grain we had left, and he was coughing and stumbling. He died the next night, and there was nothing left to do but leave him to freeze and go on. I was no longer even sure if I was going in the right direction. I must be near the town if my calculations were right, but I could see almost nothing in the driving ice particles, and I was too far gone myself to think up a strategy to find out my location. I knew that if I stopped or lay down, I would never get up again.*

*And then I see her, dimly but unmistakably through the snow. She is sitting in the light of an oil lamp, staring into the flame. I keep staggering towards her through the flurries of ice crystals. She is all I am still aware of and I move towards her as if we are in some other reality. I know I must be dying, but some other part of me registers that I am moving between buildings at last, though the town is completely deserted. Some force moves my semi-conscious body through the alleys to our house. With the last vestige of my will power I open the door, see her sitting in the light of an oil lamp. Then I fall inwards unconscious.*

*When I come to I am lying in bed. I am naked, and she is warming me with her naked body, warming life back into me. I can smell her skin and her hair. Everything is of a miraculous intensity. "This is love," I think. "Now I know for all eternity what love is." I had gone from her with another woman, and yet she stays alone in the town after all have fled so she will be there if I return. She warms me back to life. She asks for no explanations, there are tears of joy in her eyes as she holds me, she accepts me back without reproach. She speaks very little, but I see love in her eyes.*

*This is all that is of relevance in connection with that life. We had a magical winter in the deserted town, ransacking empty houses for stored food, and living only in each other's eyes. My wife got pregnant that winter, and when spring came we joined relatives of hers who lived as nomads. We had four children, and lived hard but fulfilling lives. I died as an old man after falling from a pony.*

### Concluding Comments

During most of this regression my body shivered uncontrollably and my teeth chattered. I did not feel warmth until the last part when I reached my wife again. The poor therapist covered me with an extra

## The Gift of Unconditional Love

blanket, and even offered to get a hot water bottle, but the cold still dominated. Such physical manifestation of the phenomena one is experiencing in the life being looked at is common. I have even heard of a case where a woman experienced rescuing a child from a burning house in a regression, and small burn blisters came up over her feet and lower legs. They disappeared within hours however.

One of my clients experienced travelling alone through a desert with its extremes of heat in the daytime and cold after sunset. He poured sweat during his re-experiencing of the heat of the day, and shivered uncontrollably when reliving the nights.

It is notable that although I had chosen the theme of jealousy, the deepest impression left by this regression was the total lack of it, the feeling that I now knew what it was like to be on the receiving end of unconditional love. It is interesting what our Higher Self offers us in answer to our request to view a certain life.

In the space between lives, while at one with my expanded self, I recognized that the being who had been my Mongolian wife in that life was now Bernd, the dear friend who was busy minding my baby daughter at home in my present one. As our beings communicated with each other between lives he/she had said "I'll always be there for you." I returned home to find him minding the baby and cutting up vegetables for lunch. He was, indeed, still there for me.

Although he was now 6 foot 4 inches tall and blond, I could clearly see the features of my Mongolian wife in his. Our deep but matter-of-fact friendship has been one of my greatest joys in this life.

# CHAPTER 7

## Knowing the Mind, Knowing the Body

Life with Rainer continued to be difficult. He was jealous of my friendship with Bernd, which made me feel hurt because I was convinced of our innocence. Quite apart from his resentment of my friendship with Bernd, and my torment over the whole Hildegard business, we were struggling to live happily but constantly brushing each other up the wrong way. He was away a lot giving seminars, and we tried hard to adjust to each other when he got back. But I felt resentful that he had only changed our daughter's nappies a few times since her birth, and that apart from ironing his shirts ready for the next trip away, I was of little use to him.

I admired his work pioneering accelerated learning, and I helped him by writing courses, preparing course material, and leading courses. We had started up an accelerated learning institute together – that had linked us. But since our daughter's birth, I no longer had time to work there, and he had gradually let go of that project and begun working in management training, a field I didn't share. We wanted our relationship to work, but spent a lot of time feeling we didn't suit each other. When I wanted sex, he had to work or was tired. When he wanted sex, I felt he was insensitive and fat.

Rainer had eczema on his thighs, and I hated him scratching it at night and waking me up. And he, of course, found it difficult to sleep beside me. I understand now that he over-reacted to my heightened sensitivity because his mother, in the war years, had bordered on insanity, even threatening to drown him and his brothers as toddlers in her struggle to come to terms with life after her husband's death as a conscientious objector. Probably I awoke the same old dread in him. In any case, I did this regression to the source of our difficulties.

### *Past Life Experience*

*I am standing at the railing of a pagoda in the palace grounds. It is the 13th century in Korea, and my father is the local ruler, a rather weedy but erudite man. I am his only official child, and he dotes on me above all else, even though I am a girl. My mother died when I was nine, and my father is not interested in the children of his concubines. There are only three such children anyway, and they associate mainly with the servants. My father is more interested in scholarship than in*

## Knowing the Mind, Knowing the Body

*women, and it tickles his pride and warms his rather withered heart that I, too, like to indulge in this privilege of the aristocracy. In spite of being a girl, I have access to all the realm's manuscripts, and good teachers.*

*Someone is storming along the path that runs down the hill and crosses over below the pagoda. It is my father's general, and he does not notice me. He is so enraged that that he is muttering aloud to himself, gesticulating wildly. "Fool of a girl," I catch. "Stupid old man." He gives a swipe through the air in his agitation. "What about the borders if I'm not there!" He rushes on down the path, snarling and muttering, looking very warlike in his thick leather breast and back plates.*

*I smile smugly to myself. So, Father has spoken to him. And Father's word is law. I am the only one who can twist Father round my finger when I want to. He has remonstrated with me for days, trying to dissuade me from my plan. But see, he has given in, and the general will have to accompany me. A little thrill of satisfaction runs through me. What an adventure! I decide to go up to the palace and hear from Father how the talk went.*

*He receives me in his study. He is agitated by his own decision, and perturbed by the general's ill-concealed dislike of the task, but he softens and mellows at my obvious delight. He enjoys seeing me happy. I pour his*

# TIME AND TIME AGAIN

*tea and, to show my gratitude, am very attentive to all he wishes to tell me.*

*My plan is to travel to a sacred lake I have learnt of. Behind the lake is a cave in which a giant black snake is said to dwell, a serpent of great age and infinite knowledge. According to the teachings I have found, if the serpent accepts one's offering of cooked rice and milk, one receives miraculously his infinite knowledge. Of course he can also kill humans, so normally food is lowered to him from above the cave. But I wish to confront him face to face. I want his knowledge. There is only one drawback - the lake lies well within the boundaries of a neighbouring state with whom we have been at war on and off for decades. This is why I need the general.*

*I have talked again and again with my father about the necessity of having the general accompany me. Even my father could not command that a large contingent of our soldiers be sent into the neighbouring state just to clear the way to the sacred lake for his daughter. The councillors would not believe that the investment of human life is justified for this goal, and I cannot venture there alone and unprotected - I am used to having people take care of me. So I have finally persuaded my father to let me go if the general accompanies me as a bodyguard. The fewer people who go, the less our intrusion will be noticed. It will only take a few days anyway.*

## Knowing the Mind, Knowing the Body

*The general is famous for his valour and his skill in combat, and he is a man of honour. There is no thought that he would lay a finger on me. If anyone can get me safely through enemy territory and back again, it will be him. We will go disguised as commoners. But he is furious and humiliated that he has to go off and neglect his military duties on the whim of a girl. He will do it because it has been requested by my father, who is his commander. But he feels degraded and abused (although he cannot say this), and is in a terrible rage.*

*Nevertheless, two days later we set off. The general treats me with cold correctness at first, but as I carry out his wishes meticulously to ensure our safety, some of the rancour fades from his eyes. By the third day he even gruffly praises me for my ability to squat beside the path like a peasant girl with downcast eyes when an official unexpectedly passes by on a horse. His praise fills me with an unexpected wave of delight and makes me blush. Although I am twenty three, I have had little contact with men except at official functions, and my father is too fond of me to be in any hurry to make a good political match for me. I watch the general secretly, especially when he thinks I am asleep.*

*The next afternoon we come in sight of the lake and lie in hiding for another day so that the general can observe our surroundings and decide when it will be best to approach the cave. He has to get the bowl of milk for the snake - not so easy if his accent is not to give us away - and locate a boat to get us over to the mouth of the cave. There are steep cliffs near its entrance. He decides we should attempt to reach the cave before dawn the next day, as the lake is covered with a dense mist in the very early morning which should hide our movements. He has discovered a small boat hidden under some willows.*

*Before the first breath of dawn we slip through the clammy, dew-drenched reeds to the boat. I am clutching my bowl of milk and a small box of cooked rice. My heart is beating fast, and for the first time I doubt the wisdom of my plan. The general pushes off the boat, lying on his belly in it and paddling as silently as possible with his arms so there will be no sound from paddles. But still the water makes little splashes. We reach the cave entrance abruptly in the mist, the boat grating on the stones.*

*I clamber out onto the smooth pebbles, and at first can make out nothing in the near darkness. Then I hear a sound like a faint rasping, as if a heavy roll of silk is being drawn across sand. I strain my eyes then draw in my breath as I see the dense presence of the serpent gliding down from a ledge and approaching the mouth of the cave. His head is slightly raised, his tongue flickering as coil after coil of his massive, black body oozes down from the ledge. His body is as thick as a palm trunk. I am very afraid. I force myself to bow and, putting down my offerings on a stone, I back away from him. I hear a faint sound from the general, but I am mesmerised by the snake. I have to see if he accepts*

## Knowing the Mind, Knowing the Body

*my offering. His head is by the bowl, he flickers his tongue, then lowers his head into the bowl to drink.*

*I turn in delight to the general, catch the look of horror in his eyes, and look out through the thinning mist to the edges of the lake. It is almost entirely surrounded by armed men standing practically shoulder to shoulder. We have no choice. The general steps out of the boat and, snatching my hand, something he has never done before, he pulls me around the snake and into the depths of the cave. We clamber in the darkness further and further back.*

*After about half an hour of climbing and stumbling over the slippery rocks in the dark, we see shafts of light in the distance. There are holes surrounded by ferns in the roof of the cave. The general lifts me up, and with no thought of decorum, I clamber onto his shoulders and pull myself up into bright airy jungle. Somehow the general manages to heave himself up and also scramble through the hole. There is a shock of bright light and space after the dark of the cave. Huge trees form a roof of green above us through which the sun sends columns of light. The air is soft and lush and full of bird calls.*

*We start to run as fast as we can through the undergrowth, knowing that the soldiers must be aware of this exit. We realise the hopelessness of our situation, but I have never felt so alive in my life. We pause, and suddenly, in a flash of attunement, we start*

# TIME AND TIME AGAIN

*to claw at each other's clothes, biting at each other's lips, tasting the sweat, panting, moaning, possessed by our desire for each other. Half standing, the general pulls open my robe, and I reach between his legs as if I had been doing this all my life, and ease him into me, crying with pain and delight. We fall to the ground, and it is soon over, but the wonder of it still surrounds us. We say nothing as we quickly adjust our clothes. As we move on, I feel the warm trickle of sperm and blood down my thigh. We look into each other's eyes, and we know each other.*

*As we hurry on, the world has changed; we have become part of the jungle, part of life. There is little sense of time. Is this the infinite knowledge promised by the snake?*

*Not long after this, a party of soldiers finds us. The general fights with the expertise and desperation of a doomed man, but it is six to one. When they slash his throat his blood arcs out and sprays the leaves. Part of my heart dies at the same time.*

*They take me prisoner, and bring me to their camp. When they find out who I am, they drag me to the enemy ruler who takes me as one of his concubines. This is, of course, an insult to my father. He tries to fight to get me back, but without the general his men lack real leadership and courage, and he loses a part of his realm. I produce some children for his enemy, and live as an outsider among his servants. When I am older, I am demoted to being a common servant.*

*I ponder whether I have received all knowledge. Maybe I have come to know all there is to know - the dry but satisfying exercise of the mind as I had known it in my life in the palace, and this unquestionable wisdom of the body as I had found it with the general. But there is a numb sense that there is something beyond that again, although my spirit is too broken to seek it. I die middle-aged, having little will to live, and believing I will meet the general again after death.*

## Concluding Comments

One of the most remarkable results from this regression was the almost instant healing of Rainer's eczema. He had been, of course, the general in the regression. Although it was I, not he, who did the regression, and he did not even know about it till later. His eczema vanished within days of the past life work and did not return. Truly, we are all connected. So if entangled energies are made conscious and resolved in one area of our lives, it will subtly affect all those connected to us. We should never doubt the collective value of clearing up our individual lives.

The regression made many aspects of our relationship understandable, particularly the fact that although we were attracted to each other, he felt endangered if he came too close, and experienced something like panic at the idea of taking on responsibility for me. He also had a strong aversion to my father. Accepting each other with all our strengths and weaknesses was our aim in this life. At different times we both pushed the other along the path of development – he through making me aware of the Findhorn Community, where a lot of my spiritual growth happened, and through introducing me to the work of the Bulgarian superlearning inventor, Dr. Georgi Losanov, through which I learnt to trust the impulses which come in relaxation. I served him through pushing his buttons around trusting women, and he helped me learn about jealousy – a lesson I did not appreciate at the time.

Rainer and I finally parted when our daughter was three, and he married two more times. We respect and value our connection to each other through our daughter.

## CHAPTER 8

# Flying Neolithic Style

If the Divine is a loving force, why does it allow us as humans to suffer such terrible difficulties and pain? This is a question I have asked myself again and again. That we have been given free will seems cold comfort at the time of suffering. Even ice-cream and sex seem doubtful rewards as compensation for all the hurdles we have to overcome while in a body. In every life we have to experience death one way or another. If we are the "directors" in the "film" of our lives, why did we give ourselves such frequently horrendous challenges? Isn't this taking the idea of karma to absurd lengths? To what extent does our inner focus prescribe our ways of experiencing? After we have experienced our death in a regression and have expanded into the realm of the soul, we gain some insight into these fields. Attempts to find the answers to these questions have apparently always occupied humanity. I had a chance to experience a method which may have been used in Neolithic times.

# TIME AND TIME AGAIN

It occurred as a past life "flash" under unusual circumstances, and without any theme being set. I was attending a weekend workshop led by Professor Felicitas Goodman from the University of Alabama. She had been invited to Heidelberg, Germany, as one of the speakers at a conference for psychologists. This remarkable woman, who was 80 at the time, had dedicated her life to the scientific, measurable investigation of spiritual states of consciousness. She was a tiny little woman with her hair scraped back in a bun, and she had agreed to hold a workshop for a few privately invited participants on the weekend after the conference.

The workshop was based on work she had done investigating postures found in ancient sculptures all over the world. These postures are very simple, for example, standing with the feet parallel and close together, the right hand resting on the left shoulder, or kneeling with the fingers pointing straight ahead on the thighs. Some of these postures are consistent, no matter what culture they are found in. Before Felicitas' work in this field, the explanation was that people had not been capable, in former times, of portraying the human body in more realistic poses.

Felicitas however, tested the hypothesis that they were accurate records of ways of entering changed states of consciousness. She tested numerous people who took up these postures meticulously while she shook a Native American rattle (high intensity sound) for quarter of an hour. She found a great degree of consistency in the experiences of the participants, depending on the particular posture they had taken up, for example, experience of flying, of going under the earth. The posture we were trying out when the following experience took place was one which often calls up visions containing flying, although we were not told this prior to experiencing it.

## *Past Life Experience*

*I am a little afraid of the whole situation, as this is the first time I have been guided by Felicitas' method. We are holding a simple standing pose, and have not been told what it might induce. I decide to resist it, or go into the experience gradually, so that I do not lose control. I have no chance at all, however, of retaining control. As the rattle starts I am yanked out of my body through the top of my head like a champagne cork out of a bottle.*

*I find myself standing in a circle of Native Americans who are in the midst of a ceremony. I am an elderly man with wavy, grey, shoulder length hair. I seem to be the medicine man of the tribe, and we are calling up the spirits of the ancestors and associated animals as the tribe needs guidance in a crucial issue.*

*Without warning a warrior, our war chief, springs into the ceremonial ring. He is wearing only a loin cloth and a feathered headdress, and his face and body are vividly painted. He holds frenzied eye contact with me, and is dancing wildly, passionately, stamping and springing and invoking a heightened state in all of us. I recognize him as my second son in my current life.*

*The scene changes, and I see the same warrior chief the next day, now dressed in a simple cloak. He and I are setting out from the village on a quest to find the answer to the great question before us. The quest is about our relocation in the face of approaching danger. The people of the village gather to farewell us as we set off to ascend the sacred mountain.*

*On top of the mountain (the scenery looks as if we are in the High Sierras) the chief calls an invocation and suddenly makes a sweeping gesture outwards with one arm, as if he is throwing something. I am quite unprepared for what happens. In that moment I am catapulted out into the sky as an eagle. I feel the air rushing past me, hear the sound of it in my pinions and hear my own wild call. I can see right out over the mountains to the plain beyond, and to the distant ocean. The village is tiny below me. I call again and circle up towards the sun, higher and higher, as if I will melt into the Knower, the Great Spirit.*

*And then I know the answer to the quest. It is symbolized by a fish I see far, far below me in a lake. I dive like a meteor down to the water, and rise again*

## Flying Neolithic Style

*clutching the fish in my talons. I fly back and lay the fish at the feet of the chief. It is accomplished.*

*I see my old man's body lying curled up on the ground beside the chief. I seem to be unconscious, or asleep, or dead. The eagle is gone, but the fish is lying, still shiny and wet and with talon marks on its sides, at the chief's feet.*

### Concluding Comments

This was an amazing and completely unexpected experience. It felt as if I had landed in a past life, and it is the only time I have experienced myself in one as an animal. On other occasions I have been able to attune to animals and apparently experience as they do, but I have never been one so clearly. I have occasionally had clients who experienced animal lives, however, and one woman even went into a life as a tree. Several have seen themselves as nature spirits or dwarves. If we look at this as part of the Hindu and Theosophical philosophy, where souls pass through incarnations first collectively as plants and animals, then differentiated into individuals as humans, it makes sense that people could experience themselves as animals in past lives. I would have thought the development as nature spirits or dwarves might rather lead to the angelic stream of evolution, but there are exceptions to everything.

I have felt an affinity with eagles ever since this experience and they seem to be aware of me on the odd occasions when I have been privileged to be close to these amazing creatures. My second son, whom I recognized as the Native American chief, has a shamanic side to his character in this life too. He has trained to be a firewalk instructor, could use circular breathing when playing the didgeridoo although he was never taught to do this, and enjoys rituals connected to nature.

To return to Felicitas' experiment, after each postural "round", she noted down the experiences of the participants who had been holding the pose while being bathed in the deafening sound of her rattle. The visions reported by other people at the workshop were not so spectacularly clear as this one for me, nor did I hear reports from other participants which were part of a coherent past life story, though many of them did contain elements of flying. Perhaps the ability to use the skill of "inner" flying was trained in pre-historic times through these postures, as a means of gaining access to the answers to the mysteries of life.

# CHAPTER 9

## Scholarship versus Experience

Answers to the mysteries of life come to us in all kinds of ways, and past life experiences are one of them. Of course memories of past lives occur without doing formal regressions, as we have already seen. In fact such memories are probably far more common than most people think. How often has it happened to you that you have seen a poster or photograph of some foreign scene and have been filled with longing to go there, or had the feeling that it looks very familiar? How often have you been in a foreign country but noted a deep sense of feeling at home there? Could these be ancient memories?

"Falling in love at first sight" would perhaps be better referred to as "recognising at first sight". I think we all know situations where we find ourselves telling a "stranger" things that we have not even told our best friend because there was such a deep sense of empathy with that person. In a similar way we come across people that we instantly dislike or mistrust.

## TIME AND TIME AGAIN

The following past life experience occurred spontaneously, evoked by an interesting alignment of outside stimuli. It is not the only time that my surroundings have brought up "memories". Old spiritual centres such as Stonehenge, the cathedral at Worms, and parts of Glastonbury called up strong images to name just a few. At these locations, however, I did not switch realities so completely. In contrast to the places just mentioned, the following spontaneous regression happened at a site which had no connection to my memory, and for part of the time it was a complete switch of realities.

It occurred when I was in Greece near Thessaloniki attending a shiatsu course. It was summer, and because of the extreme heat during the day, we had decided to meet for our lesson at 6 o'clock in the morning on the beach, which was bordered by a steep cliff into which steps had been cut. We each brought a blanket to keep the sand off our bodies as we practised, and a mat to work on.

Having not slept very well the night before, I was still half asleep when I arrived on the beach for our lesson, and we started the class with relaxation exercises, so that I was in a rather trance-like state. At that point something almost unheard of in a Greek summer happened – it started to rain. We were told to retreat to a room at the top of the cliff.

## Scholarship versus Experience

Dazedly I started to walk up the steps cut into the cliff, my blanket slung cloak-like over my shoulders and my mat rolled up under my arm. About a third of the way up the steps, I switched realities and I found myself as follows.

### *Past Life Experience*

*I am an elderly, white haired man carrying a parchment roll under my arm and wearing a light cloak over my robe. I am walking slowly and with dignity up the steps between the university buildings on the hill behind Alexandria. It is shortly before the time of Christ, I think.*

*I then see myself seated on an open terrace with a circle of pupils, young men in their early teens. I am expounding philosophy, and we are discussing, and referring to a rolled manuscript.*

*The scene changes, and I am looking out over the town from a doorway of the university buildings. The town is being sacked by the Romans and grey columns of smoke are rising from numerous buildings. Two Romans with helmets on, short swords held in their hands, come running up the steps – young, muscular men, sweating, with their pulse beating visibly in their necks. They are intoxicated with destruction and a sense of their own power. They do not give a fig for my knowledge.*

# TIME AND TIME AGAIN

*They pause for a moment as I take a step towards them – my age and dignity are imposing in their way. But the soldiers do not want to turn from the wave of destruction they are riding. One of them thrusts his sword up under my ribs. I smell his sweat as I fall dying to the steps. The soldiers run on.*

## Concluding Comments

My shiatsu teacher noticed that I was in a strange state, and let me sit in a corner of the room while I completed this process. Such spontaneous switches do seem to endorse the idea that, as time is an illusion, all lives are happening simultaneously and realities are interchangeable.

The lesson I learned from re-visiting this life in Alexandria was that the flow of life and death is infinitely more virile than any of the theoretical knowledge about it. As a scholar there I was wise, and had devoted years of my life to the pursuit of knowledge, yet in that moment of intensity just before my violent death, I lived in a heightened awareness of what life is that took me far beyond my teachings.

A similar awareness came to me in a life in which as a young Serbian girl, I was raped by a group of men. In spite of all the personal suffering and social persecution that I went through as a result of this violent and horrifying experience, the most lasting impression it left with me in the longer perspective was of the utter power of the sexual impulse, something that overrules our logic, our best intentions, our conscience, our laws, our judgements, often even our sense of spirituality. It simply IS. Procreation simply IS. Sexuality simply IS. Of course this in no way excuses its misuse.

## CHAPTER 10

## Light and Darkness

The last two past life experiences sprang upon me unexpectedly. This one was sought, but had some unexpected features. It was puzzling because it was the response to my request to do a regression to the life which held the origin of my distrust in this life, but I did not get a clear sense of the country, nor the time, though it was a semi-desert area and the word Sumer came to mind. It seemed almost to take place in a parallel universe. Perhaps it is symbolic. I don't know whether it can be called "real" or not. When experiencing it, I certainly felt everything to be just as "real" as in any other past life I have looked into.

### *Past Life Experience*

*I am a young woman of perhaps 16 years, the daughter of leaders of a community which lives in dwellings cut into the cliff sides in a rather arid land. The rock is a*

## Light and Darkness

*pleasant reddish-orange colour. The cliffs form a natural circle so that the area enclosed by them is the common meeting ground of the community. There is an easily defended entrance leading into this compound. Gardens and workshops are further away, and people go out there in the day time to tend the gardens and make necessary artefacts. They return in the evening, sweaty and grubby, bearing fruit, vegetables, tools and artefacts.*

*My parents and I have olive skin, dark hair and large dark eyes. We wear long pale garments. We are held in special regard in the community because we belong to a long, revered line of beings who are able on occasions to allow a strong divine energy to flow through them. Through "diluting" and focussing it, we make it available to others. There are certain places on our land where this energy flows, but if ordinary people stand there, they die, because it burns them like strong electricity.*

*To me it is completely natural that my parents and I can channel this energy, and that I am never allowed to leave our dwelling without guards. We are precious in the way that a source of water is precious – if anything were to happen to us, this source of divine energy would no longer be available to the people. So I have been guarded and cared for since birth. I am an only child, and have only recently become old enough to channel the energy in public as my parents do. We only do this on special days.*

# TIME AND TIME AGAIN

*On this day, I am escorted to one of the places where the energy flows, and I take up position seated in a niche in the rocks. A path leads around the curving side of the cliffs and past the niche. Just below the niche is a crevasse which splits the path, so a kind of hanging bridge about two yards long has been built into the path to span the gap. The people can only see me and feel the energy while they are crossing this little bridge; otherwise the curve of the path hides me from their view.*

*A special invocation is called, the horns are sounded, and the people begin to file slowly along the path and across the bridge. I must only sit there and allow the energy to flow through me and out to the people. A quiet, aware focus is all that is required. I remain completely impassive, though vitally aware of the flow. What happens to people when they enter the projected energy field is unpredictable – some are healed, some die and are pulled away, some are stunned or overwhelmed, some seem unmoved, some laugh with joy, some cry. Whatever is appropriate for each individual happens. I am not emotionally involved, although I am intensely aware of each reaction.*

*I sit for one or two hours, then the horns sound again. I step out of the niche and, accompanied by my escorts, return to our dwelling.*

*But that night I am restless. I have heard talk that there is another force in action, a dark one, just as ours is a*

## Light and Darkness

*light one. It is perpetrated by a man who has come to live in the valley, who is said to be a powerful magician. I have asked if we can visit him, for I am curious about his energy – but everyone looks horrified at the idea. The thought of seeing this man fascinates me however, and in my mind I play out schemes of how to arrange this.*

*I have decided to wait until all are asleep and then creep out alone and see if I can find where he lives. I tell myself that I will only go close enough to feel what his energy is like. I can do this from some distance. I simply want to know the "taste" of his energy, I don't need to see the man himself.*

*At last everyone seems to be sleeping. I am drowsy myself, but I steady my flagging resolve and manage to slip out of our dwelling unseen. It is not so easy getting out of the entrance to the compound, as there are guards but they are focussed on preventing anyone entering, not leaving, and I manage to slip stealthily out while they are talking. I set off down to the valley. This is the first time that I have been out without my guards, and I feel a thrill of excitement. I am a little afraid in the night, but the stars are brilliant and a slice of moon casts some light. This part of the path leading to another settlement is familiar to me.*

*It is surprisingly easy to find the opening to the cave in which the magician lives; it is as if his energy is calling me. The energy waves are slow and heavy, with a spicy,*

# TIME AND TIME AGAIN

*thick quality to them. I decide that, seeing I have come so far so successfully, I will just peek around the entrance to his cave before returning. This is a mistake.*

*As I slip with pounding heart into the entrance of the cave, I see the magician. He is seated on a huge dark carved chair, and is wearing a robe woven of many colours. He has protruding, dark eyes and a moustache, and he is wearing a brightly coloured flat cap. He is obviously delighted to see me. It is as if he has been expecting me.*

*I seal off my energy borders as I have been taught and go to step back outside, but he only laughs at my efforts. His energy is far stronger than I believed possible. "So, my little dove," he say in a throaty voice, "you have come to my bait," and he begins to pull me towards him with his energy. I resist as strongly as I can, but on his territory a strange dullness has come over me, and scalding fear wells up.*

*I call telepathically to my parents, but have the feeling that my energy has become ineffectual and weak in his presence. He plays with me as a cat plays with a mouse, letting me almost escape out of the entrance and then pulling me back with his energy. He does not touch me physically, and no-one else is present. At last I am so exhausted that I cease to resist, and fall on my knees at his feet, suffocating in his energy.*

*"So," he says, "you wanted to experience darkness. Now you can get to know it until nothing else exists."*

## Light and Darkness

*He makes a movement and a trapdoor I hadn't noticed before opens. I fall into a pit and a lid closes over me.*

*I remain in this pit until my death some days later. I experience panic, attempts to collect myself, despair, violent physical struggle, mental calls to my parents, resignation, striving, and timelessness. I begin to dry out. At some point as I stare into the utter darkness, I realize that it is made up of countless points of coloured light dancing in a way that makes them look black. This dance is very beautiful, very alive. I see darkness and light as two pyramids touching along their bases. I see that there is a constant exchange of energy between the two. As I die, it is beautiful to feel myself being drawn back into the light again.*

### Concluding Comments

It seems that a large part of my distrust in my current life was based on a deep fear that "the dark side" would overwhelm me if I relaxed my guard. The realization that in their essence dark and light are related and in constant exchange, was balancing. Now I seldom have the feeling that I have to "protect" myself from outside energies. I stand more firmly on the earth.

This "story" has something of a myth or fairy story about it, and touches the old theme of earthly existence – duality. Although it felt just as real as any other past life while experiencing it, the classic confrontation of dark and light forces is archetypal. And interestingly the regression ends with the understanding that both light and dark are aspects of wholeness.

Although I had deprived my community of an irreplaceable source of energy through my disobedience and consequent death, my youth and the innocence of my curiosity seemed to make the main learning from this life the greater understanding of the oneness of all things.

# CHAPTER 11

## Leadership and Responsibility

Duality, duality – how it plagues our existence on earth. In this regression, the experience explores finding the balance between ideals and what we call reality.

Much of my practical work on past life regressions occurred during my participation in the "Lightwork Training" courses in Germany. These were run by my teacher and friend, Rhea Powers, and her then husband, Gawain Bantle. The courses were extremely popular, and were attended by hundreds of Europeans.

The decision to attend these courses was one of the most important decisions of my life. Through the courses I discovered that many of the subjects I had heard about in Theosophy such as channelling, past lives, and ascended masters were not just amazing things experienced by a select few, but were accessible to "normal people". We did not just talk about past lives on the courses, we did regressions and experienced our past lives. We did not just talk about the possibility of people or places being influenced by disembodied spirits, we learnt to send these spirits back to the light. We did not sit in awe of channelled information in books, we learnt how to channel. We heard the angels sing.

True, a few participants got a bit lost and went on some detours on their way to the Light. But in general the courses were enormously stimulating, extended us to the full, and woke a whole generation of seekers to their spiritual potential.

One of the aims of the training was to make us aware of anything that kept us back from fully embracing our potential as spirit manifest in matter. So one of the themes we were told to do a past life regression on was "The life in which I decided to give up my power". The aim was to have us discover what had taken away our trust in our own ability, so we could reclaim our power.

This is what came up for me.

### *Past Life Experience*

*We are somewhere in Eastern Europe. It is the early 13th century. I am a man of about 48 years, bearded, with bushy eyebrows, wavy brown hair, and piercing eyes. I am dressed in a long brown tunic, like those that Franciscan monks wear but without a hood. I am noted*

## Leadership and Responsibility

*for my ability to preach, although I have not been ordained. I go into an altered state of consciousness in which it would seem that God speaks through me. My talks have a fire and a sense of truth to them which draw people to me. I feel that I walk in Christ's presence.*

*A group of people come together to follow my teachings, and we have founded a village in which, to the best of our ability, we live in an awareness of brotherly love. We are pacifists at a time when pacifism is unheard of. The local baron, under whose rule we officially stand, tolerates us on his land, for we are industrious, honest and law-abiding. He is a cynical, cold-hearted man, short and stocky with slitty eyes, but he has kept the area safe enough in his way. He rules his underlings with an iron hand.*

*Other people tend to laugh at us for not following their ways, but they respect us too, and there is little friction. They buy our goods gladly, knowing they can trust the quality. All in all, life is satisfying, and seems to confirm what I always preach – that God will care for those who follow His ways in honesty and goodness.*

*Not far from our village is a small mountain which always inspires me. I climb to the summit when I seek guidance, and it was here that I first felt that God was calling to me. It is half a day's walk to the top of the mountain, and it means crossing the river on whose*

# TIME AND TIME AGAIN

*banks our village stands. There is a rather flimsy hanging bridge across the river.*

*Today I am troubled. The baron has ridden into the village with a group of other armed men on horseback. They stand in our central yard, their horses uneasily stamping and snorting, their harnesses clinking. He calls me out to him, and I can smell the leather of the saddles and the sour sweat on the men. He tells me that word has reached him that marauding hordes from the East are moving towards us, laying waste to the land, stealing , and killing all they see. They are thought to be only days away from us, and he is calling together all men of the district to fight against them. Women and children can take shelter within the walls of his castle, which the men are preparing to defend.*

*I tell him we will not fight. I tell him that the Lord will defend those who obey His laws. His arguments do not move me.*

*"You are a fool," he shouts at last. "It's not only your mangy skin that's in danger. It's all the people here. And I need every man I can get."*

*"We will not fight," I repeat.*

*"Then die," he cries, and spits on the ground at my feet. They turn their horses and gallop in anger and dust out of the village.*

*The people who have overheard what he said gather around me. Alarm is in their eyes, and they argue the*

## Leadership and Responsibility

*matter back and forth among themselves. They look to me for guidance. "I will go with the men to the mountain tomorrow," I say. "We will pray for guidance and protection."*

*We leave before dawn so that we can be back late the same day. It is a long march, but we can do it if the older people stay behind. On top of the mountain I call to God as never before to protect His people. We pray for guidance, and the answer comes clear to me, "Thou shalt not kill. Love thy neighbour as thyself." We feel relieved and strengthened in our faith, purified and clear. We set out on the long march homeward, prepared to hide from the invaders if necessary, but not to fight.*

*As we descend from the mountain the sky darkens and a violent storm tears at us. Before we reach flat land torrential rain is sluicing down, lightning crashes into the ground all around, thunder rips open the sky and deafens us. We can scarcely walk against the wind, and decide to take shelter in a deserted barn till the sky clears. We spend a cold, wet night huddled together.*

*The wind and rain gradually abate towards morning, and as the first cold glow of dawn breathes into the sky, we set off again, trudging through the mud. About an hour later the first realization that something terrible has happened during our absence grips our hearts. We see smoke on the horizon where our village lies. It does not look like the smoke from cooking fires.*

# TIME AND TIME AGAIN

*We tell ourselves at first that lightning perhaps struck in the night, but we know in reality that the rain would have extinguished the fire. There are too many sources of smoke; the fires must have been lit since the storm. Our hearts cold with dread, we start to run.*

*By the time we reach the banks of the river it is all too clear. The village has been sacked by the invaders. The bridge has either collapsed in the storm, or been hacked through. Even at this distance we can make out bodies among the ruins. Guilt seizes me. Were it not for my advice the innocents might still live! I told them we would be protected. Oh God, my God, why have you forsaken me! How can I believe in life if I can not believe in Thee!*

*The men, some stony faced, some in tears, are trying to join strips from their clothing to make a rope. If they can get the rope to catch on a stump across the river, they might be able to cross. The river is a raging, yellow torrent from the floods of last night. My heart is a raging torrent of despair. I throw myself into the river and drown.*

## Concluding Comments

Killing myself was not wise. I could have overcome my despair and stayed with my followers. In the realm between lives, as I am in contact with my Higher Self, I realise that it would have been the next learning step for me to stick with them and work through the horror

## Leadership and Responsibility

of our experience. However, I made the choice of giving up.

Nevertheless, after returning to the light after my death in the regression, and connecting with my soul consciousness, I experienced relief beyond measure as I began to grasp that I was not responsible for the deaths of the people from "my" community. Everyone has free choice, and everyone chooses the learning experience they have. For various karmic reasons they chose to experience a violent death in that life. (Perhaps to balance out some violence they had delivered unwisely at an earlier point, perhaps to teach the perpetrators, through their deaths, the infinite value of a human life.)

At any rate, at this level of awareness they were at peace with what had happened and with me. I could stop punishing myself. It was alright to "talk" to God.

After this regression it felt a lot safer when I allowed myself to channel for others, although it is still a jump in faith each time for me. When people enquire about a channelling session with me, I often find myself encouraging them to find their own truth through various therapy forms, rather than have the answers given to them from a higher source. I also warn people that no matter what I may say in an expanded state of consciousness, the decisions they make are their own. I recommend that they should only accept channelled suggestions that resonate with their own hearts.

## TIME AND TIME AGAIN

That being said, with one exception, which was not a life or death situation, I have never experienced anything I channelled that did not prove to be correct. In the cases where I have had feedback, I have been amazed and relieved to learn that even things which seemed improbable when I said them have come about. And when I give up my resistance and allow myself to channel, the sense of impersonal compassion in the expanded state is very beautiful.

# CHAPTER 12

## Regression Transcript

To give a more accurate experience of a regression, rather than offering it as a "story", I decided to include a transcript of an actual session.

This is the transcript of a past life regression that I did on behalf of a dear friend who was dying of cancer. I would not normally recommend doing regressions for other people. In this case, however, she was too weak to do it herself, and I was desperate to help her any way I could, so I contacted my own Higher Self, and then her Higher Self, and asked that I be allowed to do this for her in order to free her of her suffering, either so she could recover, or that she could die peacefully. I requested this as a gift of love for her.

The topic I decided to experience for her was "To look at, and be released from, the karmic source of her cancer in this life."

In the transcript I have omitted the introductory relaxation part. Since the facilitator who agreed to help me with this regression was not experienced in this form of work, his responses are sometimes rather wooden as he is using a script. I have changed the names of the people mentioned. The transcript begins at the point where I step into the other life.

*F = Facilitator*

*K= Kayla*

*F. Look at your feet and tell me what you see.*

*K. They seem to be yellow, yellow shoes with points on them. Pointy shoes of some quite shiny material like satin.*

*F. Look at your body. Notice what you are wearing.*

*K. It seems to be a robe. It's largely white, with panels of embroidery on the front. Um, there are beads sewn into the embroidery.*

*F. Look at your head and shoulders. Are you a man or a woman?*

*K. At first I thought I was a woman, but now I think it's a man, it's some kind of a priest...who is wearing, because of some festival occasion, this robe. I think it seems to be a man, and he has white skin, a bit old, a bit fat. Has a sort of a yellow hat on his head. A sort of stiff, sort of square-like hat. Yes.*

## Regression Transcript

*F. What's your name at that time?*

*K. (Hesitating) Habakkuk.*

*F. Is that your full name?*

*K. I'm known as Habakkuk.*

*F. What's the modern geographical name of the place you are in?*

*K. It's got something to do with Russia, I think. I don't know if it's quite Russia. It's south, more to the south.*

*F. South East? South West?*

*K. More to the South West. Poland? No, to THAT side of Poland. Not so far from it*

*F. And what year is it, according to the modern calendar.*

*K. What comes up first is 1667.*

*F. BC or AD?*

*K. I think it's after Christ.*

*F. Take a look around, and notice where you are standing. Outside or inside?*

*K. I'm at the doorway of some important building. There's going to be a procession. I've got a long stick in my right hand. It's part of my special clothes.*

# TIME AND TIME AGAIN

*F. What are the details of the landscape if you look out?*

*K. It's in a town. It's stone. It's made of stone. I think maybe this is a church, or belongs to the church where I'm standing. I'm very powerful. They are quite afraid of me. I'm quite important.*

*F. Can you see the people?*

*K. Yes, they have their good clothes on. Some of them. There are some children just looking in between the other ones. Other people will be walking behind me. (Pause).Oh, I think some people are going to be burnt.*

*F. What is your position in the society or group?*

*K. I'm the highest member of the church in that area. I'm sort of like a bishop or something like that.*

*F. What are you responsible for in that job?*

*K. Well I'm very powerful. The people of the State can't really do anything without my support. They know this. They kiss my ring.*

*They can't ... I have all the riches of the church and I'm very good at knowing how to make people do what I want them to do. I have a sort of overview. They are quite weak, comparatively. There are some older men who work with me, and there is some young...er... like a prince. He's quite*

## Regression Transcript

*young, and he's officially the head but he hasn't really got much power. And these other men just do everything. And they work with me.*

*F. What is your attitude towards that responsibility you have?*

*K. I think it's right because I can do it... I like to be able to make things run according to my plan. I'm good at it. I had to work hard to get there, and I intend staying there. I think I can rule the country. You have to be very, very strong with these people or they will throw everything down and go their way. You have to keep them in their place and you have to watch all the time and be one step ahead. And I can do that.*

*F. Allow the scene to move forward. What happened next that day?*

*K. (Big sigh).*

*F. Allow yourself to see it more and more clearly, to experience it more and more deeply.*

*K. Yes, I'm walking through the streets with these people behind me. I am going to join the state officials. It's a special day, and we are going to... some people are going to be executed.*

*F. And what happened next that day?*

*K. There is a man, um... We are sitting on a platform, the heads of state and me, in front of the palace, the building that the government uses. There are some men, three men. The people of the town have come to watch. They... I am pleased to see these men tied up. They are my political enemies. I said...I said that they were heretics. But they also possess land, and were getting too powerful. They could have upset the whole balance. The men who advise the prince, they agreed with me. We had them caught. They have been in...they have been in chains, and they have been forced to admit heresy. I know. I don't really care about the heresy much. But it's better to have them executed for heresy than for political reasons.*

*F. What happens then?*

*K. They are going to burn them. They tie them on a pile of wood. One of them, he curses me, and one of them, he just looks at me. I can see his eyes. The other one I don't care about – he's too weak.*

*F. Move to the end of that day.*

*K. Yes, the people watched them being burned. The man in the middle – he's the one I really wanted to destroy. Some of the people do not agree with what we have done. They are muttering. I return through the crowds to the house by the church – there,*

## Regression Transcript

*where I live. The people are muttering and pushing. It didn't go off as well as I thought it would. I go into the house, and send the others away, and think. I feel... I have a bad conscience to some extent. I don't know why, because it was very sensible, what I did. But I don't feel good. I go across to the church. I want to pray. I try to explain to God, but ... I have doubt. And I don't like the reaction of the people so well. I have doubt...it won't go away. It's eating around in me. I have doubt.*

*F. In that life-time, go to the event that is the source of your theme.*

*K. It was this man, these men.*

*F. Go to the moment when you decided. What was the moment that you decided to take on the theme in this lifetime? What did you decide that begins with "I'll always..."*

*K. I'll always remember his eyes. I'll always remember his eyes.*

*F. Good, what else?*

*K. The way he looked at me. I'll always remember his eyes. I'll always carry that look around. I'll always have the feeling it wasn't right. Something...it was sensible, but I'll always have the feeling I shouldn't have done it...that he had children...*

# TIME AND TIME AGAIN

*F. What else did you decide that begins with "I'll always…"?*

*K. I'll always have to be watchful. Or I'll be followed by his eyes.*

*F. What else with "I'll always?"*

*K. I'll always doubt. I'll always know something is not right.*

*F. What else with "I'll always…"?*

*K. I'll always expect them to try to get me.*

*F. What did you decide that begins with "I'll never…"?*

*K. I'll never be at peace.*

*F. "I'll never…"?*

*K. I'll never forget his eyes. I'll never be at peace. I'll never quite trust my judgment.*

*I'll never quite trust my judgment.*

*F. What did you decide that is most influencing your current reality?*

*K. I'll be punished for this. I'll be punished for this.*

*F. Move forward then, and notice the results of that event.*

*K. The people are very restless.*

## Regression Transcript

*F. The results and outcomes?*

*K. Yes, a large band of them is coming. He has more friends than I thought. They wish to speak to me. I go out onto the steps of the church. Many of my men have run away. The others have a leader and he hates me. There's a large mob, and I am afraid of them. I have less support than I thought. The leader wants to keep it in a formal state. He wants to negotiate with me. But there are others in the crowd, who just want to get me. They want power too. They start shouting. They call me a fat rat. I feel afraid. Their leader, he tries to hold them back. He says "We'll talk to him. Let it take its course." They start sort of pushing up, in waves, coming closer up the steps. I feel afraid, and I turn to go back into the church. I want to close the church. I am not dignified any more. They (sob).... I trip on my robe. Oh, I nearly make it to the door. The other man is trying to hold them back, but they come. Yes, hmm, they start hitting me. Yes, yes, they keep hitting me, and one of them has a knife, and he thrusts it into my back. They roar... (groan)... so I'm dying.*

*F. Look exactly how you are dying.*

*K. Yes, ahhh. They hate me. They hit me, and they thrust a knife in my back (groan). The blood is going down the steps of the church. They are rushing me. And I think his eyes have got me.*

# TIME AND TIME AGAIN

*F. So going to the end of that lifetime, what did you decide looking back at that lifetime?*

*K. (Urgently) I should have found another way. I should have found another way.*

*F. What did you decide that begins with "I'll always..."*

*K. I'll always see his eyes. They all had those eyes in them, as everybody does who I judged. All their eyes were his eyes. (Crying loudly and desperately).*

*F. What's there with "I'll never...?"*

*K. I won't judge any more. I'll never judge any more. I'll never hold that power. I'll never try to hold that power. I don't want to manipulate them anymore.*

*F. What else is there with "I'll never...?"*

*K. I'll never be free of his eyes*

*F. "Next time I'll...?"*

*K. Next time I'll be very humble. I'll just be an ordinary person. I won't hurt anybody. Next time I won't hurt anybody. I won't be powerful. I won't judge anybody. I'll show them I'm sorry. (Crying loudly). Next time I'll show them I'm sorry. (Crying) I'll be very humble and I won't hurt*

## Regression Transcript

*anybody. I'll show them I didn't mean to and I'm sorry (Crying).*

*F. What did you decide at the end of that life that is most influencing your current reality?*

*K. I must be punished. I must be punished.*

*F. What else should you know about that lifetime that is important?*

*K. Don't use God's name to manipulate (sobs).*

*F. Go through that death, go through leaving that body.*

*K. Yes... (Pause. Then more calmly) My mother has come to meet me (Pause). It's good to see my mother again. For her I'm alright. It's good she came to meet me. I can still see them down there, all running around into the church and fighting. Everything is in tumult, but I'm going away from it.*

*F. Find a way to move through space and time to the place between lifetimes, when you and your Higher Self were creating the lifetime we have just witnessed.*

*K. Yes.*

*F. And from your Higher Consciousness look and see what that lifetime was really about. What was the lesson you decided to learn that lifetime?*

# TIME AND TIME AGAIN

*K. To understand about power.*

*F. And what was the experience your Higher Consciousness designed for you to have in that lifetime?*

*K. To understand about power. It wasn't...when I was younger in that life, I was quite close to God. But politics became more and more important, and it was like being in a trap. I got into it and I couldn't get out of it, and I had to keep going. I thought I had to keep going (Pause). I didn't really have to keep going.*

*F. Before you entered that lifetime, call in any beings who played a significant role in the story of that lifetime.*

*K. That man. With the eyes.*

*F. Look and see what agreement you made before you entered that body.*

*K. (Quietly, in awe) He loves me.*

*F. Say that again?*

*K. He loves me. It was his gift.*

*F. How did he agree to serve you so you could learn the lesson you'd designed for that lifetime?*

*K. He agreed that I would execute him, that he had sown enough seeds of his energy to turn the tide. I would bring the country forward in some ways, in economical ways. It was of benefit. But his ideals must be taken over. He served in that way. I served in the other way.*

*F. So would it be alright to let go of the decisions you made when you were caught up in that lifetime?*

*K. I have punished myself now. He forgives me. It was arranged. He will take...there is no hatred in his eyes now. I didn't really have to punish myself. I thought I did because of his eyes.*

*F. So which other decisions would it be alright to let go?*

*K. I don't have to watch out all the time. I don't have to punish myself.*

*F. See the person that you were in that lifetime standing in front of you.*

*K. Yes.*

*F. Listen to what that other aspect of yourself would like to communicate with you.*

*K. He says, "You have served. Don't punish yourself. You have served. You have shown up."*

*F. Is there anything you would like to communicate to that former "you"?*

*K. You were very despicable in many ways, but you did some good things too. It's all right.*

# TIME AND TIME AGAIN

*F. Anything else you want to say to each other?*

*K. No, that's enough.*

*F. OK. Embrace him and let him go. So thank (your friend's) Higher Self.*

*K. Just a moment... I'm trying to see if that man is somebody that she knew in this life. (Long pause). I think it's John! I think it's John!*

*F. Who is John?*

*K. That man is now John. (The friend's son)*

*F. Which man?*

*K. The man I condemned to death. I'm not sure...I think it's John. Yes. Ok.*

*F. So thank her Higher Self. Thank your own Higher Self. That they were willing to communicate the way they did. Separate again.*

*(Deep sigh) Come back to your own Higher Self. Let all the parts of the other Higher Self go back where it belongs. So there is a clear distinction between her Higher Self and your Higher Self.*

*K. (Exhausted) Although really all our Higher Selves are together. It's her ego that I have to separate from.*

*F. Alright. Do that. (Pause) And begin to focus more and more on yourself again, your own physical body, Kayla's body in this moment in*

## Regression Transcript

*time, in Greece. Feeling refreshed, pleasantly aware of your body. See the surroundings, the olive tree. Hear the noises, the beach, the wind in the olive tree. I'll count from 5 to 1, then you'll be completely here once again.*

A few days later my friend died peacefully.

## CHAPTER 13

## Regression Technique

A warning: I do not recommend that anyone start experimenting with past life work without an experienced therapist to accompany them. There is too much at stake. Later, when a person has become used to moving safely in and out of past lives, he or she may choose as I have sometimes, to work with a recording containing the regression framework. But only do this if you feel confident and comfortable with the process. Surprises do come up.

When clients come to me because they wish to do past life work, I always have a thorough talk to them first. Through this I can ascertain whether they are emotionally stable, and whether past life work is an appropriate way of dealing with the situation they want to work on. If they do not seem emotionally stable, I will work with them in other ways until a suitable state of stability has been reached, perhaps using theta healing or work on early childhood programming. It is also important that clients are willing to put themselves into my hands, and feel confidence in my ability to accompany them. After all, I will be going "through life and death" with them, and for them to profit most they need to be willing to surrender to the process. This is only possible if they trust me.

If nothing stands in the way of doing past life work, we now need to decide on the theme of the regression, for example, "The life which holds the source of my conflict with my mother", or "The life which holds the origin of my infertility in this life" or " The life which holds the origin of my fear of heights", or perhaps, "The life in which I had the closest connection to music/dance/healing ..." or whatever. The degree of impact of a past life regression often seems to be proportional to the urgency the client feels to deal with a certain topic. After all, there are normally hundreds of lives to choose from. Vague curiosity does not carry the desire which allows for clear and powerful remembering. And to ask to see "a past life" can lead to an indecipherable kaleidoscope of impressions.

When we have decided on our theme, I guide the client into a state of deep relaxation, suggesting that they can feel soothing, relaxing golden light flowing in through their toes and gradually moving up through their body. I go gradually through the sections of the body with them, using my voice and breathing to help them sink more and more deeply into relaxation. It is important to generate a sense of well-being, safety, total relaxation, and the awareness of being part of something greater than the individual self. Before we begin, I have the client go inwardly to a place which feels completely safe to them, and ask for the support of their spiritual guidance. In many cases I will deepen the trance with techniques from hypnotherapy.

There are all kinds of ways for clients to approach the past life they are seeking. For example they can go from their "safe place" to a corridor with lots of doors in it and open the one that leads to a certain life, or they can go up or down in a lift till they come to the appropriate floor with the sought life. Or they can evoke and tune in to a certain emotion and allow it to call up the corresponding major incident in another life.

One of my favourite ways is the one I originally learned from Rhea Powers, where the client sets out from their "safe place" and finds a doorway or gateway there which they may not have noticed before. I invite them to go through it and find themselves on a path. They may find themselves surrounded by a coloured mist, and if this is the case, they should just take note of the colour, and allow it to relax them even more. I tell them that at the end of the path there is a bridge with a platform at the far end of it. They go along the path in their own time, and give me a sign when they reach the platform at the end of the bridge. This progression along the path takes a varying amount of time, but ultimately the client will indicate with a movement or a sound that they are standing on the platform at the end of the bridge.

## Regression Technique

They are about to enter the former life. I remind them to think with a clear focus of their theme, and then to take a step down from the platform onto solid ground, and look at their feet. If using one of the other introductory ways I mentioned above, I will usually also ask them to describe their feet to me first, and (as in the transcript) say whether they are wearing shoes or any other foot-covering. This immediately gives them something to concentrate on. They can tell me what the ground they are standing on looks like, and then gain an impression of their body and clothing. From this they can normally tell whether they are male or female, and their approximate age. Most frequently people tend to enter a past life regression as a young adult, though if the childhood has been particularly hard or they die young, they will enter it as a child. They normally only enter the life as an elderly person if some major challenge occurred in old age.

In addition to these initial impressions, the client will also be able to say whether they are inside or outside, whether they are alone or not, and what they are doing. I ask them to describe their feelings. There is great divergence in the degree of detail which clients are aware of in their surroundings. Some (the more visually orientated people) can describe the architecture, food, clothes and so on in minute detail, whereas others (more auditory or kinaesthetic) have only vague impressions and feelings.

# TIME AND TIME AGAIN

In these early stages I also ask them to let the year come into their minds according to our present method of reckoning time, and I ask them to tell me what country they are in according to our present-day geographical understanding. Most clients can let me know without too much difficulty where they are, what they are doing, and what their position in society is.

My role from then on is to prompt the client to progress through the life we have entered. The amount of questioning ("So, how do you feel about that?", "And what happens next?") that I need to do also varies enormously. We are looking for incidents in the life they are investigating which are particularly emotionally charged. Decisions that they made at such times of great emotional intensity will be re-encoded in their cells when they incarnate again. These impressions may be ruling their lives hundreds of years after the initial experience.

If the emotionally charged experience was a painful one, as the majority of them are, there may well be resistance to returning to the scene. We may come close to it, and then the client will suddenly say they can't see anything more, or they don't know what is happening. It is usually helpful in such cases to suggest they wind the story back as if it were a film, and then re-approach the incident. This may need to happen a number of times before the client suddenly finds themselves in the situation they had been avoiding.

## Regression Technique

They don't have to dwell on the painful memory for long, but it is important to re-experience it in all its emotional intensity, and to become aware of what decisions they made. These may be decisions like "I'll never tell the truth again", "I'll always be alone/an outcast/a rebel", "I don't deserve to have a child/to rule/to heal/to be loved", and in many subsequent lives the client will have created circumstances which "proved" again and again that the decisions they made were "right".

Sometimes too, the client may step down off the platform at the end of the bridge directly into some traumatic experience (see Chapter 2), complete with all the physical sensations. In such a case it may be wise to ask them to wind the film back and see what preceded the incident so they can experience it in context.

On the other hand, if the client is lying calmly there, but describing horrendous circumstances, it is necessary to bring them into contact with their emotions. This may be done by getting them to breathe more deeply through their mouth, by applying light pressure to their solar plexus with the joint of my thumb, and by asking them to repeat key phrases till a sudden up-welling of emotion occurs.

It could be that the client "dies" at that emotionally charged moment in the life they are re-visiting, or perhaps the life progresses to another emotionally charged occurrence, which can also be accessed as described above. But at some point, then or later on, I will guide them to the day on which they died in that life. I ask them to tell me how they will die, and who is present (if anyone).

They can look back on the life they have just lived and say what was particularly important in it. They then go through the experience of leaving their body. There is no need to draw this out longer than necessary, and in the case of a slow and painful death, it may be necessary to encourage the client to move on swiftly. In any case, they will usually report that they can see the scene of their death from above, an indication that they have left their body, and it is obvious that they are suddenly peaceful and pain free. Often they are aware of a bright light which they feel drawn to move towards. Sometimes a relative or dear friend who has passed away prior to this death comes to "pick them up" and accompany them into the light (see A Regression Transcript). Sometimes a light-being emanating love appears to guide them.

My role now is to encourage the client to move further and further into the realms of light, allowing the light to expand them till they feel they are close to their Higher Self or Soul. This is where the healing really happens. I ask them what this life we have just re-visited was really about.

Normally, when a person is living a life with all its emotional upheavals, they do not understand its deeper significance. From the point of view of their soul, however, the life is meaningful, and was chosen for the learning experiences in it. When this is deeply grasped, the feelings of being a victim or a perpetrator disappear, and with it the sense of guilt or victimhood. A person can see that they chose a certain fate for a reason. They can see that the events were chosen to give them a chance to make meaningful choices.

If, for example, they have been feeling terrible because they just killed someone, they will understand that their "victim" chose to experience that particular death for their own karmic reasons, and that they agreed to be the perpetrator for their own reasons. There is a tremendous sense of relief from this awareness. It is usually possible to call in the being who has shared the recent dramas with them, and for them to view them with loving awareness and understanding, pointing out, or perhaps asking them, what their learning experience was. They no longer feel threatened or ashamed before them.

I can ask whether the life had therefore been a success from this wider perspective, and normally they will say that it has, at least partially. They may see clearly what it is that they wish to learn "next time". It is now that I usually also ask them if they recognize any of the people in the past life as people they know in their current life. Very often they will recognize one or two of them, as we tend to incarnate again and again with individuals from our soul group.

# TIME AND TIME AGAIN

Before they return to their current life and waking awareness, I suggest they call in the being that they have just been, and see that former self at a short distance. They can ask him or her if there is a message for them. Such messages are usually short and full of compassion. The client also has the possibility of giving a message to their former self, even if it is only to thank them. They then take leave of each other.

I now ask them to find a way that feels right to them of travelling through time and space, till they find themselves standing before the life that they are currently leading on earth. The client is still in an expanded state of awareness, so I repeat the question I had asked them in connection with the past life we had been viewing, but this time I ask it about their current life: "What is this life really about? What is important now?"

Here too, the answers are usually simple, profound and true. Before we return to normal, waking consciousness, I ask if their Higher Self has a message or gift for them in the form of a symbol, a phrase, a colour, or a teaching. The client may be feeling a little tired by now, but the response is usually touching and meaningful, though its full significance may not be immediately clear.

We then thank all our guides and helpers for their support, and ask them to help the client to integrate the new knowing into their everyday life with grace and

## Regression Technique

ease. I count from one to five, having let the client know beforehand that this will bring them back to waking reality. They are encouraged to breathe more deeply and energetically as I count, move their hands and feet, stretch, and then on five, open their eyes, "feeling refreshed and ready for the rest of the day".

We have successfully completed a past life regression.

After we have talked a little about their experience, and the client has had a drink of water, and got used to moving again, they can go out into the everyday world. I remind them to treat themselves gently for the rest of the day, and assure them that they can ring me if anything comes up that they need to talk about. Sometimes clients draw a picture of their experience as soon as they get home, or write it down while it is still fresh. If they asked for that, we will have taped the session anyway. Life goes on, but probably with a new awareness.

In the early phase of my own experiences doing past life regressions, I always asked a colleague to accompany me during the regression. I would certainly not suggest that anyone attempt past life work without a qualified therapist with them. Too much can happen to risk stepping into these areas alone and inexperienced. However as I became more conversant with the field after doing quite a number of regressions, I would sometimes regress myself using an audiotape

# TIME AND TIME AGAIN

with the cues of the various stages of the technique on it.

After the children were in bed and I had unplugged the telephone, I would lie down in the spare room, the light dimmed, and follow the tape, putting myself into deep relaxation. I would then follow the cues on the tape, but keep my finger on the pause button. If I needed longer to process something than the tape allowed, I would press pause, work through whatever it was, then press pause again to continue. Although I did a lot of successful regressions that way, I far prefer having an accompanier I trust with me. Then it is possible to relax more fully and enter into the experience more deeply.

It is perhaps wise to remind yourself that in the greater context, everything we experience is a dream. Learn from the experiences of past lives, but do not cling to them. Let them help you, but do not use them as an excuse.

Good luck on your journey.

# CHAPTER 14

## Concluding Thoughts

When I first read the chapters through consecutively I was impressed to realize that in the majority of the lives, I am striving to learn, teach or lead. Even in the "love" stories, I am looking for knowledge and attempting to align myself, if belatedly, with higher laws.

Is this the human condition? Is everyone basically striving to find unity, express divine love, and return consciously to the Source? And is everything else that happens simply due to errors in judgement? False ideas about what might make us happy? Misguided expressions of free will? Explorations of the dark side so as to be more aware of the light? Addiction to intense feelings?

I have recounted lives which I found particularly interesting and meaningful, and which I thought might interest others. One of my reasons for writing on this subject was because I felt these stories were so amazing. I once said "I couldn't think up stories like that if I tried".

And yes, of course I have looked at numerous other lives of mine. They include being a Tibetan monk, an Indian temple dancer, a Roman soldier, an Eastern European Jewish girl, a German prince, a Greek woman dedicated to Athena, an early Christian in Rome, an Egyptian High Priestess, a Maori woman in pre-European New Zealand, and many, many more.

One of the things that I wonder about is the realisation of how slowly I have grown. Realizations or skills that I have gradually mastered in one life do not automatically flower from birth in following ones. Rather they seem to have to be painstakingly re-awakened. Moments of near-enlightenment are followed by daily struggle. But it is all VERY, VERY interesting, VERY, VERY intense. Maybe we are just addicted to the intensity? Maybe the time has come to find intensity in bliss instead of pain. And in the long run, the stories do not matter. They are scenarios that we played out, learning fields, ripples on the ocean of awareness.

Perhaps we are simply allowing the Divine Source to experience everything through us. Perhaps when so much has been experienced we can decide that it is part of the human task on earth to live in bliss and fulfilment, and bliss and fulfilment are what we will manifest. It will be rather fun incarnating then, won't

## Concluding Thoughts

it? Though maybe by then we will have moved on to other dimensions....

The main thing to know and assimilate now is that we are infinitely more than any past or present life. We are part of the Divine essence, experiencing, and moving on back to itself. We are Divine bliss incarnate, learning through leaving bliss behind, experiencing deeply the loss of it, and then reawakening consciously over time to the possibility of living in Divine bliss again. Here and now.

Blessings on your path.

## Books You May Find Helpful

Dethlefsen, Thorwald, 1984, The Challenge of Fate, Coventure Ltd, UK

Dethlefsen, Thorwald, 1976, Voices from Other Lives, M Evans, UK

Lipton, Bruce, 2005, The Biology of Belief, Mountain of Love Productions, Santa Rosa, CA

Newton, Michael, 1994, Journey of Souls, Llewellyn, St.Paul Minn

Newton, Michael, 2001, Destiny of Souls, Llewellyn, St Paul Minn

Newton, Michael, 2004, Life Between Lives, Llewellyn, St Paul Minn

Newton, Michael, 2009, Memories of the Afterlife, Llewellyn, St Paul Minn

Tucker, Jim B, 2005, Life before Life, St Martins Press, New York

Weiss, Brian L, 1994, Many Lives, Many Masters, Piatkus, London

Weiss, Brian L, 2004, Same Soul, Many Bodies, Piatkus, London

## About the Author

Kayla Mackenzie-Kopp grew up in New Zealand and Samoa. After completing a B.A. at Auckland University, she left for Europe, and "accidentally" stayed there for thirty three years.

Along with bringing up three children, she taught English at Heidelberg University, had her own practice for spiritual psychotherapy, worked as a channel and reincarnation therapist, and gave seminars on a wide range of subjects, from angels, to fire walking, to Family Constellation Work. She learned by doing and giving, and has worked with hundreds of people.

In 2002 she returned to New Zealand, and now lives and writes on Waiheke Island. You can contact her on kaylahello@yahoo.co.nz

www.ingramcontent.com/pod-product-compliance
Lightning Source LLC
Chambersburg PA
CBHW061657040426
42446CB00010B/1779